STOP WASTING MONEY!

Using Mary Hunt's simple, responsible wisdom, thousands of people nationwide have already turned their finances around—without sacrificing their standard of living or their dignity. Recognized by *Business Week,* the *L.A. Times, Newsweek,* and John Naisbitt's *Trend Letter,* her timely advice shows you how to:

- Slash grocery bills
- Avoid the coupon trap, the rubber-check syndrome, and the deadly impulse-buy
- Use cheap home remedies to improve your family's health
- Use everyday household items to make safe, effective cleaners that cost only pennies
- Manage mortgages to your advantage
- Raise financially responsible kids
- And much more!

**St. Martin's Paperbacks titles
by Mary Hunt**

THE BEST OF THE CHEAPSKATE MONTHLY

THE CHEAPSKATE MONTHLY
MONEY MAKEOVER

THE BEST OF *The*

CHEAP-SKATE MONTHLY

SIMPLE TIPS FOR LIVING LEAN IN THE '90s

MARY HUNT

ST. MARTIN'S PAPERBACKS

THE BEST OF THE CHEAPSKATE MONTHLY

Copyright © 1993 by Mary Hunt.

Back cover photo of Mary Hunt by Jay Erselius.

ISBN: 0-312-95093-4

Printed in the United States of America

St. Martin's Paperbacks edition/May 1993

10 9 8 7 6 5

ACKNOWLEDGMENTS

There have been few times in my life when I have felt more challenged than immediately following a phone call I received five months ago. A female voice on the other end of the line left me with a question: What is a literary agent? I was a newcomer to journalism. My entire career could be summed up in five issues of my infant newsletter, *Cheapskate Monthly*. I had spent many years in real estate, and an agency was not an unfamiliar concept. I was able to pick up the literary part without much difficulty, but what the heck was a literary agent?

Within a matter of weeks the phenomenon of *Cheapskate Monthly* continued to develop and there I was agreeing to write a book—start to finish—and I would have four months to do it. Yes, a whole 120 days! However, my initial panic subsided when I took a few minutes to analyze the situation. I follow directions well and knew I would find great solace and security as soon as I got my hands on the "How-to-Write-a-Book-in-120-Days Training Manual and Field Guide." It didn't take me long to realize that such a document is hopelessly nonexistent and my only comfort at that point was that perhaps I had stumbled across the title of my second book!

ACKNOWLEDGMENTS

During the four shortest months of my life I have learned that I am able to accomplish things far beyond my own perceived limitations and that my friends and family have more confidence in me than I have in myself. While many were spectators cheering from the stands, others were cheerleaders performing incredible feats to make sure I finished this project. To them I owe a debt of gratitude:

To Cathy Hollenbeck, my assistant, secretary, manager, appointment rememberer, proofreader, media expert, confidence builder, fan and wonderful friend—thank you for your patience and support.

To Toni Lopopolo, my literary agent who took a big chance on a long shot and patiently explained to me just what a publisher is. You stretched me beyond my wildest imagination and I will be eternally grateful.

To Jennifer Weis, my editor. Thanks for making a neophyte feel so welcomed. Thank goodness your passion and enthusiasm are so contagious.

To my two sons, Jeremy and Josh, (a.k.a. "Matt" and "Jim" to *Cheapskate Monthly* readers) proud members of the next cheapskate generation who weren't the least bit surprised when I announced that I was going to try something new. You both are my pride and joy. I'll love you forever, I'll like you for always.

And last, and certainly most important, to Harold, the love of my life, best friend ever, business partner, head cheerleader and strong supporter. Thank you for having confidence in me when I felt the least confident. You refused to give up on me and I will spend the rest of my life thanking and loving you.

CONTENTS

CONTENTS

CONTENTS

THE BEST OF *The*
CHEAP-SKATE MONTHLY

WARNING

What you are about to read may change your thinking about the unbridled use of credit cards and compulsive debting. It is possible, and hopefully probable, that you will be convinced to stop using them altogether. Furthermore, reading the following material may indeed persuade you that there is a way to live beneath your means; that you can learn to spend less and begin to save more. Living from paycheck to paycheck may soon be a thing of the past.

You will be invited to consider the benefits of reducing your expenses, increasing your savings and simplifying your life through the adoption of simple tips, helpful hints, practical solutions and ingenious substitutes.

INTRODUCTION

WHAT IS *CHEAPSKATE MONTHLY?*

Before we go any further we need to talk about one thing. This word *cheapskate*. I have a feeling you are not all that thrilled about the term, and frankly neither was I. But as you will soon learn, the life-style of a spendthrift turned out to be all but totally devastating for me. I made a change. I became a _____ (fill in the blank). See? There is really no word that nicely describes the opposite of a spendthrift. *Cheapskate* has a little zip to it and I decided I would just redefine the word! After all, isn't the dictionary just someone's opinion? In *my* opinion, *cheapskate* now describes a very classy and dignified individual who saves consistently and spends less than he or she earns. Makes me want to take on the entire English language! Let's see . . . "root canal" will mean "Caribbean cruise," "traffic school" will mean "vacation". . . .

Back to this cheapskate thing. It is this philosophy

that became the impetus for my newsletter and what this book is all about—living within your means.

Cheapskate Monthly is a full-size, eight-page newsletter that is dedicated to bringing *dignity* to the art of living within one's means. I hate to break this to you, but true dignity cannot be found in the number and color of your credit cards.

Think of *Cheapskate Monthly* as a support group by mail. A monthly nudge to keep on spending cautiously and saving wisely. A regular "atta-boy!" for your desire to live free of consumer debt. The heart of the newsletter is the information about practical hints, tips, secrets, and even some pretty wacky ways to make things last longer, to use less and to come up with cheaper substitutes. By using this information and encouragement you may well be on your way to breaking free of your financial bondage.

Living paycheck to paycheck, worrying yourself sick that you are about to lose everything, feeling driven to keep up with your friends and neighbors will soon be a mere memory because you are going to learn hundreds of money-saving ideas to put into practice today . . . and forever. There's no time like now to start reaching for financial peace of mind.

When you are ready to join the *Cheapskate Monthly* family, look at the back of this book for a subscription blank. If it has already been taken, you can subscribe by sending a check or money order in the amount of $12.95 for a one-year subscription to:

CHEAPSKATE MONTHLY
P.O. Box 2135
Paramount, Ca 90723

Living within your means is no longer just a dream—it is possible and I am going to show you how!

> **cheapskate** n. chēp-skāt; a wise and dignified person who spends money cautiously, saves money consistently and always lives according to his income.

CHAPTER 1

From Credit Card Junkie
to Cheapskate

My Story

I used to be anything but a cheapskate. I would break into a cold sweat at even the thought of being considered cheap. And I was driven to making absolutely sure that a very clear line of demarcation was drawn between my world and those pitiful souls residing in the land of Cheap. I could outspend anyone and I charged my way through life feeling quite entitled because I had every charge card known to the English-speaking world.

It all started quite innocently with a promise. As a child, I was a daydreamer, a future-planner. I grew up embarrassed that I had to wear hand-me-down clothes and things purchased at the secondhand store. I, the Scarlett O'Hara of the fifties, vowed that I would never be poor and that my children would never wear clothes from the thrift shop. There! Just like waving a magic wand, I guaranteed my adult status and that of my children. If only I had been wise enough to make a similar vow regarding a way to pull it off.

Within days of my wedding, I cautiously suggested to my new husband that perhaps we should look into getting a gasoline credit card. After all, we were now in a different social stratum and every real family must be prepared for unforeseen emergencies. We needed to get with the program and stop depending on cash so much. We needed plastic! Harold went along with the idea and before I knew it we received two shiny new credit cards, one bearing my name. Wow! "Free" gas whenever I wanted! No longer would I have to dig around for loose change in order to pump a few gallons into my car. I could fill up whenever the mood struck and I knew that never again would I have to be concerned with mundane issues like the price of gas. I had clout and it felt good. Being a married woman was quite prestigious.

It seemed only logical that we should have an alternative brand of gas available (just in case of emergencies) and so we went for a second set of cards. After all, if one is good, two should be better. These came more quickly and with less effort than the first. I could feel our status soaring to new heights and I carried the proper credentials to prove it.

By the time the babies came along, the first credit cards had been canceled by the gasoline company. We had been late with our payments quite a few times and had even missed some along the way. Now who would've thought a big company with all that money would demand that we pay them back . . . in full . . . every month? Not to worry, though. In addition to a nice assortment of gasoline cards I had added every department store card in southern California.

It was so easy. If a particular store didn't automatically send me a preapproved set of cards in the mail, all I had to do was pick up an application in the store. It became a game not unlike collecting baseball cards. I was compelled to acquire every charge card available. You must understand that I never applied for the cards because of any specific purchasing plan, but rather for the security I thought they would bring to our lives. I rationalized that we needed them in case of emergency. Little did I know that the very things I believed would provide security were to become a catalyst for crisis.

Harold was soon promoted to middle management with a large, prestigious California bank. I could not have been prouder! One of the items in his benefit package was a totally unsolicited handy new device—a bank card with a very nice line of credit. Now, not only was I "entitled" to all the gas I could use, the department store cards and the bank card prepared me for any kind of unforeseen need. And unlike the gasoline companies, the others didn't require full payment. These companies were quite pleased to allow a small monthly payment; in fact they all but pronounced a blessing over me every time I used them.

Soon I found my life filled with many little emergencies. Often these emergencies were manufactured from my poring over department store ad magazines which would show up in the mail. My overactive mind and impulsive tendencies would join forces to convince me of an urgent need. I would become privately fixated on a certain item and be unable to relax until I found a way to get it. I felt a certain, albeit temporary, high when I bought the latest in kids' clothing or GI Joe "men" for my boys. I felt greatly justified in spending huge sums in fabric stores. I would buy everything needed for project after project, the justification being that I could make all kinds of clothes and decorator items for much less than ready-made. In reality, very few of the projects ever materialized and the goods became obsolete, eventual donations to the less fortunate.

And the best part was the more I used those cards and continued paying the minor monthly minimums, the better standing and status I had. Why else would they keep increasing my limits? When the bank card limit reached the four-figure mark I just knew they thought I was fantastic. And I was certainly keeping my promise. I was not poor and my kids did not wear clothes from the thrift store. We showed real well!

Shopping became easier in the seclusion and comfort of my home. With a phone in one hand and a mail-order catalog in the other I was able to create Christmas for myself and my children any time I had a whim. I realize now that I was attempting to go back and fix my own childhood by giving my children all the clothes, toys and attention I missed. I was trying to fill a void by giving gifts which were bigger and better than the recipient could believe. I was making up for what I lacked, fulfilling my vow that my kids and I would never be poor and that I would always have the approval and acceptance of my friends—even if I had to buy it. I lived out the only agenda I knew: External appearances are all that is important. Anything going on inside that conflicts with a perfect facade must be ignored, denied and put aside.

My instruments of entitlement were not limited only to credit cards. I had a checkbook. While I considered credit card spending to be long-term deferment (like hundreds of years from now), writing checks was short-term deferment. Often I would neglect to record checks I wrote. It was safer that way because Harold couldn't track my spending. His unobservant temperament became my ally. I could all but redecorate the entire house and he wouldn't notice.

I worked under the philosophy that somehow by the time the check was ready to clear I would magically come up with funds which I could sneak into the bank. Of course it never happened, but still I would write checks, often with reckless abandon. One of two things happened over and over again. Either I would overdraw the account or bring the balance down so low that when Harold went to pay bills there was no longer enough to get us through the month.

Writing rubber checks is bad enough, but to add to the mess, Harold was the bank manager! Let me assure you that this kind of behavior from employees is not looked upon kindly by your average financial institution. Imagine his embarrassment and rage when one of his staff would have to sheepishly advise him of the situation and suggest that he make an immediate deposit. The phone calls I would receive during one of those incidents are not among my most pleasant memories. And you think *your* blood runs cold when the bank calls!

More than once Harold's job was in jeopardy, and still I couldn't stop my outrageous behavior. I was not making enormous purchases—we're not talking new cars or even new furniture. I was five-and-ten-dollaring us to death.

Inwardly I felt frail, weak and insignificant. The act of spending gave me momentary sensations of power and strength. I would temporarily feel cared for and nurtured. These were wonderful feelings and I made sure I experienced them often. As time went on things were getting pretty sticky, especially around the first of the month. I had incurred such heavy consumer debt (all those credit accounts pulling down interest rates of 18 percent and up) that our monthly expenses exceeded our income. Fortunately for us, or so I thought, we were benefiting greatly from the real estate booms of the seventies and eighties. Each time we got too far behind we would just refinance the house, pulling out our precious equity, plunging ourselves deeper and deeper into trouble. And of course the higher mortgage payments would eventually put us right back where we had been. We bought into the debt consolidation theory: Take out one big loan to pay off all the small ones resulting in one smaller payment each month. What a terrible mistake that was.

Our difficult financial situation prompted Harold to consider a career change. An ordinary man would have considered something quite different, but this extraordinary man refused to give up on me. An opportunity came along to try self-employment and he jumped at the chance. He said goodbye to the bank and his paychecks and we took another financial plunge.

Together we made some crucial blunders. We were driven by the fantasy of getting rich quick and we went into a business about which we knew nothing, doing so with borrowed funds. It is no wonder that in four short months our first entrepreneurial attempt ended quite abruptly with a devastating business failure and the loss of all the money which had been temporarily entrusted to our custody. (Isn't that a lovely way to say "loan"?)

Our debts were enormous and our income nearly nonexistent. We were both unemployed and the pain became unbearable. I was terrified because I could see no way out. I had run out of ways to deal with the emergencies. We had all of the elements required for a divorce—bankruptcy, loss of our home and destruction of our family. I was desperate. It was only when I hit absolute rock bottom that I was willing to consider a change.

I vividly recall that Saturday afternoon in 1982 when I was alone in my mother-in-law's kitchen. I fell onto my knees, begged for God's forgiveness and made a new promise: I would stop my totally irrational spending and debting and would seek a means by which to climb out of this financial pit. I had to change. There was no other way. Ashamedly I realized that I had much more control over my spending than I had ever wanted to admit. I no longer had to convince anyone, including myself, that I wasn't poor.

I needed to start making some major financial contributions to this marriage partnership. I had made far too many withdrawals. Willing to do anything, (fear is a great motivator) I accepted a full-time job. Now this was no ordinary job. With my real estate license I was able to combine property management with sales providing a steady income plus commissions. Good thing too, because Harold decided he needed to stay home for a while and become the newest "Mr. Mom." I became the breadwinner. What a turn of events! We immediately cut out all day-care costs. Two little boys got to spend huge amounts of time with their dad and I was relieved of the pressure that many working moms experience because Harold took over the household. We switched roles and it was weird. Believe me—I adapted quickly. Being scared witless was probably the best thing that could have ever happened.

Sure, we had to teach ourselves about frugality. It didn't come naturally by any means. We were shocked at how much we were able to cut back. But the most amazing thing is that no one really noticed —including the kids. It just goes to show that others are not nearly as impressed with our artificial lifestyles as we think they should be.

Gradually, as we were able to reverse our spending habits, we began to get out of debt and our drastically reduced living requirements became our way of life. Things went so well that in 1985 we were able to go into business for ourselves in a more practical and sensible way. With backgrounds in banking and real estate we opened an industrial real estate company.

None of this happened overnight. And we are still not completely out of debt. We may never be free of the scars and effects of the past. We will always wonder what might have been had we not been so financially foolish. But one step at a time we are making progress. The light at the end of the debt tunnel is becoming brighter. And I am still learning that my dignity and self-worth cannot come from possessions and cannot be dependent on the number of credit cards I can produce.

We did not file for bankruptcy, our marriage has been strengthened by the tremendous challenges we've faced, and we didn't lose the house. We've learned to save money and our two sons have grown into fine young men who have learned financial responsibility right along side us.

After struggling for ten years to not only make ends meet every month but to also make significant repayments toward those massive debts I had run up, in October 1991 I became very impatient with the snail's pace the whole process was taking. My impatience drove me to try and think of some way I could increase our income in order to get this repayment thing over and done with. And quickly! We have better things to work for and frankly I was really sick of living with the pathetic mistakes of the past breathing down our necks month in and month out.

Trying my hand at writing a newsletter seemed like a good idea. I certainly had a timely topic, lots of material and having an office already established, I was pretty much set up to start another business. The writing part was an unknown but I felt confident enough to at least give it a shot. Having mastered the effective business letter, I figured a newsletter would have some of the same characteristics—just be longer.

And so on January 1, 1992, *Cheapskate Monthly* was officially launched. It received a surprisingly positive response from readers across the U.S. and Canada.

God has taken the unlovely mistakes and blunders in our lives and begun to weave a tapestry of unbelievable beauty. I cannot express how thankful I am.

Cheapskate? Who me??!! You bet!

CHAPTER 2

The Debt Mess

Head Over Heels in Debt

No one is born in debt . . . yet. I suppose the day
will come when as each baby comes into the world
he or she will be weighed, measured, fingerprinted,
given a social security number, and assigned a right
and proper portion of the national debt. Thank-
fully, that day has not yet arrived. Sadly, most of us
have managed to incur significant debt all on our
own.

If you are an average American you have four
credit cards. These plastic items have become the
standard passport into the vast world of shopping
centers, electronic and catalog mail order, restaurants, transportation, and now, amazingly, super-
markets and grocery stores.

For some reason we have come to accept that if
the application is approved, the amount of the
credit extended represents entitlement. If the auto
loan is approved it's as if a mandate has come from

on high assuring us that this is certainly an afford-able purchase! We are a nation controlled by debt. Unsecured consumer debt.

So just exactly what is "debt"? Debt is what results when one person owes money to another person, place or thing. I suppose in the strictest sense of the word, owing "a cup of sugar" or "your deepest grat-itude" could be construed as a debt, but for now let's just limit it to money. Generally speaking the words *debt* and *loan* are synonymous. I, however, pre-fer the philosophy which distinguishes the terms as follows: A *loan* involves tangible collateral or secu-rity. A *debt* is unsecured and involves a promise, an understanding. Charging clothes at a department store incurs debt. If you fail to make a payment the authorities do not come out and repossess the arti-cles. The debt is unsecured.

So you see, the difference between a loan and a debt has nothing to do with your honor, intent or good faith. There are certain things over which we have no control and circumstances such as unem-ployment or illness occasionally arise, making repay-ment impossible. In the case of a loan, the lender simply takes back the collateral and the loan is con-sidered repaid. In the case of a debt, the creditor is out of luck. Your promise to pay is worthless and he is left with no choice but to come after the debtor's credit rating.

Excellent financial principles throughout the ages are like the laws of nature—universal and unchang-ing. To "owe no man anything" has always been the preferred way to live; the borrower is always the servant to the lender. Unsecured consumer debt places the debtor in bondage and as the amount of debt increases, the weight and power of those shackles that bind the enslaved tighten even tighter. We only deceive ourselves when we acquire goods and services through the use of credit cards and unsecured loans. We pretend that these things are liberating us —making our lives fuller. The truth is that we are just digging a pit, then jumping in and covering ourselves with the weight of the debt. While we would be quick to concur that our good sense and heart's desire is to provide an income stream for the future, we are doing just the opposite!

We spend every cent we have and when there isn't enough (like every month!) the credit cards bridge the gap. And for the 72 percent of us who don't pay off the credit card balances every month, the debt begins to build. And the next month something unexpected happens and again the credit cards become the lifesaver. And before long, paying the minimum payments becomes more and more burdensome—requiring some other creative financing plan like a debt consolidation loan or another credit card, for starters. Do you see what is happening here? We are committing our income, unearned from future months, to cover the expenses of the current month. And then it becomes next year's salary which will be required to pay this year's expenses. And it is very likely that income of the next decade will be required to cover the expenses of the current decade!

Does this sound impossible? It's not—and I, for one, know exactly how that feels—and it is the pits. Is the matter of the national debt coming to mind here? Why, our own government has modeled for us just how to spend ourselves to death.

The creation of debt doesn't always come in the form of four- and five-figure loans. Most of the debt which I incurred was done a tiny bit at a time.

Common Ways Debt is Incurred

- Taking a cash advance on a credit card
- Purchasing fuel with a gasoline card
- Requesting an advance on your payment, bonus or commission
- Paying for a meal with a credit card
- Putting airline tickets on a credit card
- Buying mail order using a credit card
- Failing to pay the rent on time (you owe it, so a debt is created)
- Making arrangements with a hospital, doctor or dentist to make payments for services rendered
- Any contract requiring a signature and installment payments

---

Nothing on this list seems out of the ordinary, does it? Millions of people "debt" in these and similar ways, day in and day out. And what's more—we are encouraged to do so! Maybe I'm too sensitive to the subject, but I'm being pressed on a daily basis to buy on credit. Take, for example, a fabulous piece of mail I received just today. Imagine this—a beautiful, slick, attractive catalog offering a fabulous new computer (which I've been eying) for 36 easy $90.00 interest-free payments! Who could resist? I'll admit it—for a few scary seconds I was relapsing into serious consideration. The advertisement was so well put together and the payment plan seemed so easy. The entire promotion was impeccably and subliminally delivered right down to the postage paid reply card and worry-free guarantee.

Not long ago we paid off another (of the many) of our department store credit cards. I got a private moment of glee imagining the horror on the face of the computer operator who entered that particular payment. I'm sure panic spread through the department when it finally sunk in that for the first time in 22 years the Hunt account showed a $0 balance. My fantasy turned to reality when within two weeks we received two brand-new GOLD cards from this store with a new and improved credit limit of $2,150. The cover form letter from the president applauded our most favored standing! This company was pretty worried that we had given up our debting practices. Imagine if all of their customers followed suit. We're talking 19.5 percent interest here! Not only did they send the new cards, they offered a 25 percent discount on the maiden purchase in addition to a lovely gift. They're no dummies—they know that if they can get me to use them once, I'll be hooked again!

Our son Jeremy recently graduated from high school and what should arrive in the mail shortly thereafter? An exciting notification that he had been preapproved for a Visa card. All that was required was his signature and that of his cosigning parents. This bank painted a very solemn picture of the young man away at college with a real emergency situation. The conclusion of the sales pitch was: Now that you're going to be away from home you need to be well prepared to face life's little emergencies. They went on to point out how expensive books and supplies can be, and how comforting it is to know that you can eliminate worry by simply accepting their credit card.

Please heed my warning. No one ever starts out with colossal debt. It starts innocently with just a few dollars owed to a friend or family member. Next comes a credit card. Tiny little balances don't seem to be a problem. Then comes another card and a few minor emergencies. Before long the debting becomes more than occasional.

Warning Signs of Impending Financial Doom

- Bills are not being paid on time
- Writing out the checks but not mailing one or all
- Checking account is rarely balanced
- Taking cash advances from credit lines or individuals
- Accepting additional credit cards
- Paying only the minimum on charge accounts
- Bouncing checks
- Borrowing from family and friends

If you are in debt, I doubt very much that it happened overnight. And so getting out won't happen overnight either. I challenge you to resolve right now that you will not debt even one more dollar. Ever. I can't tell you that it will be easy—but I know you can do it. Clearing away the dark clouds of debt will release joy, passion and excitement in your life!

Peer Pressure

Haven't you always considered peer pressure to be something that plagues children? I have always tried to teach our boys that peer pressure, if not recognized, could persuade them to look a certain way or participate in certain behaviors only because "everyone else is doing it." We think that children should have control over this dreaded conduct and by simply defining the malady they should be able to weigh, measure and make the right choices based upon their value system. We tell them to stand up for what they know is right; just because everyone else is doing it doesn't mean you have to! Or . . . if everyone else jumps off a cliff, does that mean you will, too?

Such training is probably not too effective if kids see their parents living their lives to "one-up" and "keep-up" with their friends and peers.

Just think of all the ways our lives are shaped and defined by peer pressure: How and where our kids are educated, the size and location of our homes, the model and year of our automobiles, the labels on our clothing, the magnitude and originality of birthday parties, the lavishness and immensity of Christmas and on and on and on. . . .

There's nothing wrong with those things in and of themselves; the problem occurs when debting becomes the only way to affect the acquisition. Never underestimate the subtle driving force of a credit card! It has the ability to bring terrible devastation.

Perma-Debt

Issuers of credit cards have only one agenda: to keep you permanently in debt. Their goal in life is to put out the bait (issuing the card), jerk the hook (offering you some minuscule rebate or gift on the first use) and reel you in. The rest is a piece of cake. They know that once 72 percent of you can be enticed to accept a credit card . . . use it just once . . . and they've gotcha!

Consumer credit interest rates are massive, anywhere from say 16 percent to 22 percent, with an annual fee here and an over-credit-line-fee there, here a cash advance fee, there a user fee, everywhere a fee, fee, fee—some are effectively charging more like 30 percent interest!

Consumer credit is a big-time industry. The credit card companies and banks have much at stake. Your perma-debt situation is their lifeblood and you can be sure they are quite interested in maintaining that condition.

Bouncing Checks

A checking account can be a very clever way to purchase without money. I used to do it and so I know the difference between an honest mistake and a planned, contrived manipulation. There is a law against passing bad checks. Criminal prosecution is generally reserved for persons with criminal intent or habitual offenders (is the word *politician* coming to mind). If these criteria don't apply to you, chances are you don't need to worry about being jailed for it. Also, banks generally charge pretty hefty fees for bounced checks. All it is, is unconscionably large interest to pay for what is generally not more than a few days' delay. You do have another worry, though, and that is that creditors and merchants don't, as a rule, trust people who bounce checks on them. Trust is an important thing to maintain and a very expensive thing to rebuild.

If you have never had a problem with this you are to be congratulated. If, on the other hand, you identify with me, you will undoubtedly agree that it is a shameful practice. I think the whole concept of the checking account was developed to fulfill a need for convenience and safety—not to be used as a loan vehicle. If you know the embarrassment of having an account closed involuntarily due to excessive NSF (Not Sufficient Funds) activity then you would do well to heed my advice, change your ways and commit to a life of cash spending.

Write down every transaction. I can almost hear some of you checkbook perfectionist types laughing, but there are many of us who have difficulty doing that! You see, once the expenditure is written down it becomes real. Until such time, a state of denial can be a much more comfortable place to be. As long as the current balance remains a "guesstimate," it seems as if spending can continue with reckless abandon. It's amazing how that approximate balance is rarely in the same ballpark with the real amount. So make yourself write down every check, every deposit, and the current balance—every transaction without fail. Yes, that includes Day-Night Automatic Teller transactions. You can do it. Let me put that another way. You *have* to do it if you really want to get control of your checkbook and stop bouncing checks.

The most clever among us can come up with all kinds of justification for this activity. Not only is writing Not Sufficient Funds checks wrong, it is very expensive! I have heard of banks recently who charge upward of $30.00 per incident. This doesn't include the merchant's fee. Merchants now have the right in California to charge treble damages (three times the amount of the check) up to a certain limit and report you to the authorities. It's just not worth it! Enough said.

Paycheck to Paycheck

Whenever I think of the phrase, "life on the edge" I am propelled into childhood memories involving automobile trips, great heights and narrow roads.

As Murphy's Law would have it, I was always on the side of the car closest to the . . . edge. And my front row seat gave me a spectacular view of the bottomless canyon below with its giant mouth open and ready to swallow me up in the event I dared to come one inch closer. Add to that perilous thought that I had absolutely no control over the situation, partly because of my insignificance as a child but mostly because of my distance from the steering wheel and brake. I often thought how much more comfortable I could be if I were on the safe side of the car and my brother next to the edge—that way he would go first and break my fall. (Sorry, Tim!) Not until we were safe at last on the straight, flat, boring highway could I relax and enjoy the trip. How sad that I missed so much of the beauty because all I could think about was falling off the edge.

I have no idea how many breathtaking views, how many out-of-the-way parts of this beautiful country I have seen but was unable to enjoy because of my very real, but undoubtedly unfounded fears of the edge! Fear has a way of spoiling things because of the distortion it casts across what is real. Kind of like a fun house with mirrors that can let a short person feel how wonderful tallness is, or cause terror to rip through a tall person who for a moment actually feels short and squatty!

I am certainly not saying the edge was not real. My sincere belief that we were just one inch away was probably pretty farfetched, but some profound turn of that wheel could have plunged us right over the parapet into some unknown but surely devastating destiny. I am happy to report that in all of those years and zillions of scary miles, never once did we fall off the edge.

It's no fun traveling on the brink of financial devastation, fearful of any unexpected expense which could push you just over the edge. Living from paycheck to paycheck keeps us on the edge, never having enough money to pay all of the bills and still have some left over; postdating a check or two; writing checks hoping they won't clear until you can get your next paycheck deposited; making some checks out but not mailing them until payday; committing next week's paycheck for this week's expenses; waking up at four in the morning wondering "How would I pay my bills if I lost my job tomorrow?"

Living under this kind of gloominess can be a bit depressing to say the least. The worst part is that so much energy is expended worrying and fretting that the beauty and joy of the moment is lost in the glare of stress and strain. But you don't have to live month after month feeling that if you come one inch closer you will fall and be swallowed up by the jaws of financial ruin. Here are some ways you can take steps away from the edge and onto safe ground so that you can relax and enjoy the view!

Start saving. Experts tell us that everyone should have cash put away to cover at least six months of expenses. When you are on the edge, that thought usually brings a sarcastic retort, "Yeah, right!" The goal line can seem a million miles away to someone starting on his own one-yard line. So start by having enough to cover one week, then move to a pay period and then one month. At that point at least you will have enough to live on until your unemployment checks kick in! Each time you make a savings deposit you will be backing away from the edge, and that feels so good!

Make a plan. Have a conversation with yourself and decide what you could eliminate or scale down in order to reduce expenses (finishing this book would be an excellent start). You plan for other possible disasters i.e., hurricanes, earthquakes, power outages. So make a plan for an "edge disaster!" Who knows—it might be so brilliant and logical that you will adopt it and then you will be taking an immediate giant leap back from the edge!

Stick to it. One person's extravagance is another's economy. You are the only one who can determine where your own life-style can be adjusted and how much any particular luxury is worth to you. What are you willing to give up to make it possible to continue eating lunch out every day, for instance? The secret to living joyfully on any income is establishing priorities before you spend. Then stick to it. Don't give up!

CHAPTER 3

Getting Out of This Mess!

Commit to Honesty

When your financial life is all messed up every area of life is affected! Even one's basic value system is vulnerable and open to attack. There are few areas of life that challenge our integrity as much as financial pressure. How else have such phrases come into being as "the check's in the mail," "I mailed it so if it doesn't show up, I'll stop payment and send another" or [to a department store clerk] "There must be some mistake—I paid my account in full just last week!" How about "My checked bounced? Oh, the bank screwed up my account. Just redeposit it." Need I go on? (Are you wondering how I know all of these excuses? I'm sure I originated them.)

If you're going to get out of your mess and into the black—there's only one place to start: commit to honesty. Make a pact with yourself that you are going to approach your finances with complete and brutal honesty. Let your creditors know that you are embarking on a financial recovery plan. And if you can't afford something—you can't afford it. There is nothing wrong with that. It is honest and you are going to benefit greatly as soon as you can say those four little words. ("I-can't-afford-it.") Don't let your family or yourself talk you into something that you know is not right for you.

A recommitment (or maybe for you it is a first time commitment) is going to bring you a huge sigh of relief. Finally you are going to be able to relax a bit and stop all the nonsense of trying to cover up one poor choice with a lie that requires another lie and on and on. Isn't it amazing how we can adjust our ethics according to our situation? Most of us wouldn't think of telling a fib to the PTA Committee, but are real good at just happening to forget to sign the check to the telephone company, hoping that such an oversight might delay clearance of that check by a few days.

Stop Debting

Using the word *debt* (noun) as a verb (to debt) is rather unscholarly—you won't find *debting* in the dictionary. "Debting" has come to mean the act of owing money to another.

It can be a personal loan from a parent or child; it can be unpaid rent or an installment purchase that does not involve collateral or one of who knows how many other ways of getting something without paying for it *now*. Most commonly, debting is facilitated by the use of a credit card. Consumer credit these days is rather plentiful, available in just about every retail store in the country. And the availability of that credit has plunged the majority of adult Americans into terrible debt. It has become the norm to spend what we do not have; and we are not the only ones to do it—look at our national debt. (I wouldn't dare quote a figure, for indeed it would be incorrect by the time this sentence is finished!)

But who can blame us? Everywhere we turn we're told to buy what we want *now*, regardless of whether or not we have enough in cash or savings to pay for it, let alone need it! We are encouraged to do it on credit—to buy *now* and pay (a lot more!) later at outrageous interest rates. Creditors often want to lull debtors into a false sense of security, said state of mind being conducive to buying things debtors would, on cooler reflection, see they couldn't afford.

Compulsive debting is more than just an occasional meal charged to a bank card. It is the repeated use of credit, first by choice and later by necessity. In time a big chunk of discretionary income is required to pay the minimum payments on the charge cards and so when an unexpected expense rears its ugly head, the debtor feels there is no choice but to incur yet another debt. And then the monthly payments are that much greater, causing that much more pressure—and so it goes. Eventually the credit sources will become "maxed out," but rarely in the case of a compulsive debtor will that stop the activity. A new way to debt will be found and the problem just grows and grows.

An overwhelming debt situation doesn't usually happen overnight. In my own case it took about twelve years.

There's only one way to reverse this process: Stop. The best way to make sure you stop is to cut up the cards, cancel the account and commit to the fastest payoff schedule possible. This is serious business and stopping this kind of activity may very well be one of the hardest things you will ever do. I'll not soon forget the day I was able to get the cards out of my purse and into a safe deposit vault. (I took the process in steps.) I felt stripped, naked and violated. But one hour at a time I was able to get a hold of myself and within a relatively short period of time the empty worthless feeling was replaced with one of freedom and relief.

Once you stop incurring new debt, you must also come up with a workable plan to reduce and eventually pay off those nagging credit card balances. While wishing and waiting for a big fix (you win the lottery, an unexpected bonus is bestowed upon you, you receive a sizable inheritance), come up with a realistic and aggressive payback plan. Keep in mind that you can make additional payments on your charge accounts during the month—that a creditor will accept $5 or $10 any time! So instead of feeling that those small payments are no more significant than a drop in a bucket—recognize that over a year's time they can really add up and make a big difference.

Once your debts are repaid *continue making payments to yourself!*

Saving Yourself from Compulsive Optional Purchases

- Do not carry credit cards
- Throw away all shopping type junk mail (catalog shopping, book clubs, CD/cassette clubs, makeup clubs, kid's book clubs and magazine rip-offs).
- Make a verbal commitment to your spouse, friend, parent—SOMEONE—that you will adhere to a 24-hour waiting period before making any optional purchase. Since most of these purchases are made without much serious thought, you'll find that those purchases you do make will be right and wise decisions.
- Insist on a month-to-month arrangement with your health club or other services that sometimes require contracts. This means you pay for the current month with no obligation to continue should you change your mind or something unexpected comes up.

- Develop a cautious attitude when any purchase requires your signature. Recognize this as a red flag that requires further investigation.

Start Saving

Want to know the secret to surviving during lean times or for that matter, any time? Want to know the difference between the person who is broke all the time and the financially secure person? I can tell you it is not education or social standing. It is not intellect or beauty. The answer, while simple, will completely revolutionize your life if you will just learn one easy principle: A portion of everything you earn is yours to keep. What's the big deal, you ask? You might think that *everything* you earn is yours to keep. WRONG! Right off the bat, a good portion of it goes to Uncle Sam. Next you have health insurance (I'm just going down a typical paycheck stub), unemployment insurance, Social Security. So do you think that your *net* income is yours to keep? WRONG! You have rent/mortgage, food, clothing, etc. And on it goes until every penny is gone. And what do you have to show for all of your earnings at the end of the year? If you are like the great majority, the answer is "nothing." You pay everyone but yourself! But a part of everything you earn is yours to keep. And that part should be absolutely no less than ten percent, no matter how meager the income. Pay yourself first; ten percent right off the top. After all who is more deserving? Who needs financial support more than you? Ten percent of everything you earn is yours!

If you are fortunate to have an employer that offers a payroll savings program, sign up. At the very least, arrange to have ten percent of your gross income taken off the top and put into savings. If you never see it, you probably won't miss it. And if you have been used to living paycheck to paycheck on one hundred percent of your income, you will definitely have to make certain adjustments. But before you know it you will become acclimated, provided you are diligent, persistent and honest. Should your employer have a matching program of any kind, you are indeed fortunate. Participate and take full advantage of the generosity of your company. Not everyone is so blessed.

If you don't have a payroll savings program available—start your own. Your bank will arrange to automatically take an amount you specify from your checking account and transfer it directly into some kind of savings instrument. Remember—no amount is too small. Your savings plan might well start in a sugar bowl! But if you make a solemn vow to never withdraw, soon you will have enough to invest. You don't have to have thousands of dollars to make your money start working for you.

Think of your savings as your servant. At your bidding, your servant will work hard for you 24 hours a day, seven days a week, and will never complain or require anything in exchange for undying loyalty. And soon your one servant will become two and then four and on and on. That's the wonderful result of a good investment. It's like perma-debt in reverse!

Hands Off that Savings Account!

If you find yourself wanting to "borrow" back what you have put aside to save, be thankful for at least one thing: You are completely normal! The challenge, however, is to put some space between you and the cash so you will be able to resist the temptation! Here are some practical ways to deal with yourself.

- Separate your checking and savings accounts.
- Keep your savings and checking accounts in different banks.
- Open a passbook account which will limit your access.
- Open your savings in a bank in another city which has no branches close to you. Do all of your deposits by mail. Making a trip of many miles is probably not something you would do without a lot of serious thought!

- Make a contract with yourself and someone you trust in which you promise to wait a full 30 days before making any withdrawals.
- Establish an account which requires two signatures to withdraw. .

Spending Record

We teach our children from a very young age how to respect our privacy, and as they mature their own rights to privacy are bestowed upon them. Little by little they become more self-governing and less accountable to outsiders until one day those fully matured, independent little birds are ready to leave the nest to make it on their own. Somewhere in that journey from the nest to the new nesting grounds the transfer of accountability from parent to self should take place. But in the area of finances the process must have a high breakdown rate because too many of us end up accountable to no one for our personal finances. And that aversion to accountability can be one's very worst enemy. Example: Have you any idea what your average cost for food per month was over the last year? How much you spend on utilities in the average month? Auto repairs? Cab fare? What is the total amount of money you spent last month on debt service? What percentage of that went toward debt reduction? What did you spend in coffee shops and on fast food . . .

yesterday? Don't feel too bad—the typical person has a difficult time coming up with anything close to exact figures for such routine expenses.

I suppose denial has something to do with it. If you have no idea what your bank balance is, it is easy to play games and fool yourself by adding a digit or two instead of facing the possible reality that you don't have enough in there to buy a newspaper, let alone cover the cash advance you managed to pull out of the automatic teller machine last night.

Assuming that you are sick and tired of living in a financial fog, under a black cloud of not knowing where all the money goes, then you desperately need the brilliant light that only a precise spending record will turn on in your life. You may be hesitant to bring into sharp focus the exact nature of your finances. And just like a new strong pair of eyeglasses that correct fuzzy vision, there will be a period of adjustment. You may even develop a headache or two! But you cannot underestimate the value and importance of recording your spending. Knowing the truth will set you free!

For the next thirty days, you are going to keep a daily spending record. A spending record is simply a written accounting for money spent including those funds withdrawn from the dreaded automatic teller machine! And for now this should not necessarily entail any changes in spending activity. You need to know how you spend your money—and this is the only way to find out. If you are part of a team where one person handles the bulk of the money, this is going to require a little teamwork. If you have an uncooperative partner, start by becoming accountable to yourself for whatever amount of money you control. As you become better and better at managing those funds—who knows?—you might end up controlling the purse strings; so don't underestimate the importance of adopting this invaluable new behavior.

Get yourself a little notebook or pad of paper; something small and practical. Any notion you have of carrying a full-on clipboard or three-ring binder should be dismissed here and now. This is going to be your own private matter and so the less attention you draw, the better.

Each day, start with a fresh page and put the current date at the top. Each time you spend cash or write a check, jot down two entries: what and how much. Don't neglect writing checks in the check register, too—this spending record is not detailed as to payee and account numbers, etc. That's it. One page per day, every day. No time off. No endless details and no totals (for now). Experts say it takes 21 days to succumb to a habit, so in about three weeks this activity should be as natural as breathing.

This daily spending record in itself is going to bring to light what heretofore has been a very dark corner of your life. And the light, just like truth, is going to set you free!

Typical Daily Spending Record

Date: _____

Tommy's lunch	$1.35
Coffee (2)	.50
Lunch	3.78
Grocery store	28.73
Rent	550.00
Gasoline	10.00
Jenny's school sppls	$2.34

A weekly spending record is going to bring further clarity because it is going to summarize your daily spending activities. Come up with categories in which you spent money. Don't get too complicated, i.e., "clothing" can cover every family member plus dry cleaning and alterations; but don't be too general either. "Food" could mean everything from coffee and donuts on the run to groceries and restaurant meals. More specific categories are necessary. Your weekly record should resemble the following:

Typical Weekly Spending Record

Week #1_____

Savings	$100.00
Groceries	83.46

Food (away from home)	52.73
Rent	550.00
Telephone	68.74
Gasoline	20.00
Oil change/lube	14.95
Clothing	53.87
Kid's miscellaneous (school stuff)	5.86
Gifts (Grandma's birthday)	9.58
Household Maint (Home Depot)	38.68
Magazine/subscriptions	12.95
Newspapers	1.75
Total Week #1	$1012.57

Last, you will need a monthly spending record which will be the four weekly records summarized by category with a monthly total. Take a little time and come up with a concise but detailed list of categories for your own personal situation. Not too general but not too vague. For an excellent example with clear description see Jerrold Mundis's book *How to Get Out of Debt, Stay Out of Debt and Live Prosperously*. (See recommended reading at end of book.)

There. For at least one month, you will know where the money went! Whether you are shocked out of your mind or pleasantly surprised, the facts are clear and you can consider financial denial a thing of the past. Now that your economic vision has cleared and your financial acuity has been honed, you have climbed out of a rut and are poised to make some serious progress in liberating yourself from the clutches of debt and financial bondage.

You will continue to keep a spending record as long as you desire to be financially responsible. I hope that is for the rest of your life!

Spending Plan

I hate the word *budget*. The very sound of it conjures up images of straightjackets, chains and shackles. A budget impedes and restricts. It is a cruel taskmaster; a merciless warden.

The word *plan*, however, denotes a design to accomplish something. It is a vehicle to get from point A to point B. Think of a spending plan as your own personal set of blueprints you are going to follow to construct your greatest dreams and desires; a treasure map that will direct you to your greatest accomplishments!

The next step is to determine your net income. You may receive your income weekly, twice a month, or monthly. Your spouse may be paid on some schedule different from yours. You may receive dividends quarterly, etc. Use the following to determine your average monthly income:

Conversion Chart to Determine Average Monthly Income

If you are paid weekly, multiply your weekly
net pay by 4.333

If you are paid biweekly (every two weeks)
multiply your biweekly pay by 2.167

If you are paid twice a month, multiply your
semimonthly pay by 2

If you are paid monthly, your monthly pay
equals your average monthly pay

If you are paid quarterly, divide your quarterly
pay by 3

If you are paid annually, divide your annual
pay by 12

Include all sources of income: interest, dividends, rental income, child support, spousal support, bonuses, lottery winnings (!), etc.

Your spending record gave you an excellent idea of your typical monthly expenses. But problems are going to surely come up if you forget to set aside money regularly for payments that do not come due every month. Examples: property taxes, insurance, medical examinations, auto repairs, gifts, vacations, household maintenance. List all of these kinds of things and determine an annual total and then divide by twelve to come up with the total monthly

Typical Monthly Spending Record

Month of _____

Month:	Week 1	Week 2	Week 3	Week 4	Total
Savings	$100.00	$100.00	$100.00	$100.00	$400.00
Rent	550.00				550.00
Groceries	83.46	237.65	58.60	74.34	454.05
Food (away from home)	52.73	14.50	5.76	45.85	118.84
Electricity		87.50			87.50
Heating fuel					00.00
Telephone	68.74				68.74
Car payments			279.00	183.00	462.00
Gasoline	20.00	20.00	20.00	20.00	80.00
Auto maintenance	14.95		37.50		52.45
Insurance		72.50		22.00	94.50
Clothing	53.87	89.00		12.98	155.85
Property taxes	200.00				200.00

Category					
State & Fed taxes	250.00				250.00
Private school tuition	76.00				76.00
Magazines/subs/newspaper	14.70				14.70
Gifts	9.58				9.58
Entertainment		25.00		10.50	35.50
Haircuts/Beauty salon				17.50	17.50
Household maintenance	38.68	21.53	16.67		76.88
Medical	14.25				14.25
Children's misc.	5.86		24.00	10.00	39.86
Credit card payments	158.00				158.00
Debt repayment	75.00				75.00
Miscellaneous		5.00	25.00	10.00	40.00
Totals	**$1,771.57**	**$686.93**	**$566.53**	**$506.17**	**$3,531.20**

amount you will need to set aside in your reserve account. I know this is getting scary but stay with me. We will get through it!

Look again at your monthly spending plan and take off anything that was duplicated when you determined your reserve expenses. For instance, perhaps last month (the month in which you kept your spending plan) you paid a property tax or car insurance installment. Make these necessary adjustments to your spending record and come up with a new total.

Take your average monthly income, subtract your monthly expenses (from spending record) and subtract your monthly reserve expenses. Anything left? Yes? Then you are the proud owner of positive cash flow! On the other hand, if you came up with a negative balance, don't panic. That big red total is the reason you've been having trouble making ends meet. That deficit is the reason you keep having to borrow and debt—and the debt just makes that total all the bigger because of the interest. Pretty disgusting isn't it?

This is the point that it would be easy for you to throw this book in the closet and forget the whole thing. But wait! There's more. There is hope; you can turn it around—just don't quit!

Get out a fresh sheet of paper and write the name of the new month at the top. Put down all of the categories from your spending plan (including reserve expenses). Make two columns: "Actual" and "Plan." In the "Actual" column write down the exact figures from last month. Now go over each and every entry. Does it seem like you spent too much here? Are there ways you might be able to cut back on that particular item this month? Can an essential be converted to an optional that can wait? Can you change a need to a want for a little while longer? Only you can decide. Be realistic. For instance it is not practical to think you can not eat for the next month. As you go through the categories, write down the amount you plan to spend in the "Plan" column. Total them both. Is your "Plan" total getting any closer to your actual income? Good. It is very possible that even with these kinds of adjustments, you are still going to be in the "red." There's more you can do!

There are three ways to convert your negative cash flow to positive: (1) decrease expenses, (2) increase income and (3) sell assets to raise cash to pay off debt. You have gone through the list and determined where you can cut expenses. (As you get to chapter 6, you are going to learn many more ways that you've probably never thought of.) What possible ways can you increase income? You may need to find a temporary part-time job nights and weekends. Perhaps you can perform some service for extra money such as house-sitting, baby-sitting or yard work. There may be overtime available or extra work you can do at home in your spare time for your employer. Explore every possibility—leave no stone unturned. Remember, this is going to be a temporary situation.

Once you have decreased expenses, increased income and find you still have a negative total, it may be time to consider selling assets. Every day people just like you are making extra cash by selling things they no longer use or enjoy. You can do the same. Consider consignment shops, classified advertising, yard sales, etc. You may even consider selling a vehicle to eliminate a monthly payment and get by until you can afford to buy another car for cash.

Only you can determine what drastic measures should be taken to get your life out of the red and into the black. It may mean selling your home and relocating to a rental. It may mean looking for better employment.

I challenge you to take these steps, to honestly assess the exact state of your personal finances. Think of this as major surgery. It hurts real bad at first, but recovery will be speedy and you're going to feel like a new person!

Debt Reduction Until Total Repayment

Let's review: So far we've committed to complete honesty, which will be evidenced by (1) no more debting (EVER . . . NEVER), (2) keeping a precise spending record and (3) living according to a spending plan. These are the three keys to turning around out-of-control finances.

As you faithfully make payments on your outstanding debts each month, the balances will slowly begin to come down and as you faithfully record every expenditure, you are going to start seeing a little more positive cash every month. Party time? Not yet! You need to devise a plan which will use those leftover dollars to speed up your debt reduction and eventual total repayment. Living debt-free is really possible—it is no longer just a dream.

Following are two methods for repayment of your debts. I don't feel that one is more desirable than the other—both work superbly. I prefer the latter as it concentrates on paying one debt in full at a time. I like the feeling of knocking out those debts one at a time rather than lowering the balances equally until they all zero out at the same time.

Method #1: List each and every debt; for our purposes here, unsecured debts. This would *exclude* mortgages and auto loans. Be sure to include every debt, even those loans from relatives or friends, past due rents, amounts owed to the IRS, etc. Next, determine the total amount you have each month to pay toward your debts—over and above the minimum required payments. It may be only a few dollars to begin. But as you continue *not incurring new debt* you are going to have a bit more each month to apply to your debt repayment plan.

Just for example, let's say that you owe a total of $9,500. Determine what percentage of the total each debt represents. (Divide the individual debt by the total of all debts, i.e., $1,500/$9,500=15.8%.)

Let's say that this month you have $100 for perma-debt reduction. You send 15.8 percent

($15.80) to MasterCard, $8.90 to Nordstrom, $12.60 to the IRS, $21.10 to Tom, $10.00 to Dad and $31.60 to Citibank. Doesn't sound like much more than a drop in the bucket—but that doesn't matter! This will start your repayment plan as well as encourage a positive new behavior and create a much improved attitude.

Possibly from time to time you will receive unexpected funds. If you are really committed to debt reduction, don't even think about spending it on anything else. Take the total and divide it proportionately among your creditors. Contrary to popular belief, they will accept payments more than once a month. As you see those balances decline, it is going to do something for your spirit. You will feel exhilarated and relieved that not only are you making steady and regular repayment, but you are not incurring any new debt.

Determining Total Debt and Percentage of Each Debt to the Whole

Debt owed to:	Current balance	Share of total debt
MasterCard	$1,500	15.8%
Nordstroms	850	8.9
IRS	1,200	12.6
Tom	2,000	21.1

Dad	950	10.0
Citibank	3,000	31.0
Totals:	**$9,500**	**100.0%**

Method #2: Add up all of your outstanding balances and look at them as one big bill ($9,500). Add up all of the regular monthly payments and arrive at a monthly total that you pay. Then list your bills in order, according to their payoff times—2 months, 20 months. Note: If you can't determine this by your monthly billing, call the creditor to find out exactly how many months full repayment will take if you continue to make minimum monthly payments.

Make the regular payments each month and concentrate on paying off the bill with the shortest payoff time. Let's say you have the same $100 available per month (as in Method #1) to pay toward perma-debt repayment. The bill with the shortest payoff time has a monthly payment of $36.00. You would send a total of $136 each month until paid off (the regular monthly payment *plus* the $100 allocated for debt reduction). As soon as this bill is paid off completely, celebrate only briefly. The next month take that $136 (which you have been paying on the first bill) and apply it to the next bill in line—along with the regular payment. In a much shorter period of time, that second bill will be paid off and then the regular payment for this second bill *plus* the $136 goes to the third bill and on and on. This really does speed up the repayment process. It is exciting to see those balances go down so quickly.

By adopting one of these two methods, you will soon see that your spending plan really does pay off. Even if you can only pay $1.00 per month to your creditors—it's okay. They'll take it. As you continue to refrain from debting, you will steadily have more money at your disposal. You will know how to adjust your spending and repayment plans and will actually begin living honestly and with the certainty that you are making progress and that financial freedom is possible.

You've Got to Be Kidding!

No, I haven't completely taken leave of my senses. I know that not everyone is even close to being able to realistically choose one of these methods of repayment because their net monthly income barely covers food and rent, let alone anything else! But no case is hopeless. You have to believe me on this.

I have chosen to touch only briefly on the subject of bankruptcy. This extreme course of action should be considered only when absolutely no other choice remains and only with the full understanding that it's no fun, it's going to remain with you for the rest of your life and should not be taken lightly. Any future potential creditor has the right to inquire whether you have ever filed bankruptcy. Even though it will disappear from your credit report after seven to ten years, your answer to that particular question could limit your future, especially in terms of buying real estate, for instance. I have heard from people who've shared with me the emotional toll bankruptcy took on them personally, to say nothing of the effect it had on their children and marriage.

Okay. Now that I've taken that possibility away from you, let's talk about what you can do. Let's say you have $75,000 in total consumer debt, you haven't made payments for months, are dodging phone calls and threatening letters and have been spending your days hiding from your creditors. Remember about committing to honesty. Now's the time. You have to communicate with these people. If you can't face them in person, or speak coherently on the phone, at least write them a letter. (See example following and yes, you have my permission to type it out verbatim—just be sure to plug in the correct figures.)

So how much do you have left after you pay your bare bones living expenses? $50.00? Oh, fine! And how is that going to help with $75,000 debt? It's going to get you started, that's what! Even if your letters say that you are going to pay each creditor $5.00 a month, that is where you are going to start. As you are able to relax in the comfort of honestly facing your depressing situation, you are going to become more productive. Abundance and prosperity will come your way and you are going to be so happy. But it is going to take time—after all you didn't get into this mess overnight. Lighten up and give yourself some time. You are going to be able to figure this out for yourself, provided that you are diligent and persistent. If the pain of your financial situation has become great enough and you have hit rock bottom, then you are truly ready to make a change!

Sample Letter to Creditors

January 1, 1993

The ABC Company
1111 W. Royal Ct.
Anytown, USA 99999

RE: Account 123-45-6789

Gentlemen:
I (or we) am writing to you about my account referenced above. I deeply regret that I have fallen behind and have failed to abide by the original terms of our agreement. I want you to know that I am committed to full repayment in the amount of approximately $_____.

I have recently undertaken a financial recovery program and have received assistance in assessing my financial situation resulting in a full repayment plan. I am doing everything I possibly can to avoid filing for bankruptcy.

Your account, unfortunately, is only one of many that I owe; my total debt is $_____ with monthly payments totaling $_____. You can understand that my present net monthly income of $_____ less drastically reduced living expenses of rent, food, utilities, etc., does not leave funds sufficient to pay even the minimum monthly payments to which I originally agreed.

Enclosed please find my check in the amount of $_____ which represents the amount I will be able to pay each month on my account for the next six months. At that time my situation will be reviewed. Hopefully the payments will be increased regularly to allow for full payment at the earliest possible date.

I respectfully request that the interest rate you are charging be reduced so that a greater portion of my payment will go toward principal reduction.

My financial recovery program projects that I will be completely debt free within _____ years.

I look forward to learning that you have processed this payment. If, however, you are unwilling to work with me as outlined above, kindly return the enclosed payment so that I can send an additional payment to another of my creditors who has agreed.

Thank you in advance for your cooperation.

Sincerely,

Once you have sent out these letters it is imperative that you regularly, without fail, continue to make the payments as promised. You need to restore your creditors' trust, so don't blow it now.

Give It Back

So far we have established four powerful new behaviors that, when implemented with total honesty, are going to completely revolutionize your financial life: (1) no more debting (*ever . . . never*), (2) keeping a written spending record, every day—forever, (3) faithful adherence to your own personal customized spending plan and (4) a realistic consistent perma-debt repayment plan. Each of these four absolutely necessary activities points inward, is self-serving and by itself will not provide the necessary balance you need in your life. The missing ingredient that will provide stability and meaning has to do with giving back—generosity.

We're talking about unselfishness—not self-sacrifice or self-deprivation. A principle of life is in operation here. St. Francis of Assisi put it this way: "It is in giving that we receive." It goes back to the Old Testament where God instructed that the "first fruits" i.e., the best of the crops, were to be given back to the Giver!

Speaking of crops, the process of pruning—giving something up—is absolutely necessary to ensure that trees produce fruit to the maximum not only in terms of quantity but also quality! It is also true that when a healthy person gives blood, the process stimulates the body's ability to replace, which results in greater strength.

Any body of water needs both an inlet and an outlet in order to remain fresh and vibrant. The

Dead Sea is a perfect example of what happens when there is no outlet—no flowing through. It is stagnant and dead. Sure, it has an unbelievable stash of valuable minerals but what good are those? You won't find any fish, vegetation (except some major bacteria) or recreating in the Dead Sea. Having never had the privilege of visiting it, I have to believe reports that it is pretty foul and often stinky. Not a real lovely thought.

Generosity, giving back, demonstrates one's regard for the well-being and happiness of others. The absence of giving in one's life will restrict and retard the process of becoming free from debt.

If you feel you don't have enough for yourself, let alone some to give away, you are not seeing the big picture. It is when you feel the neediest that you should give the most. There's nothing like seeing the needs of others to get your eyes off your own seemingly dismal situation. Anyone can afford to give—even if it is as little as a nickel! And giving is not limited to our financial resources. You can give your time and your talents. Believe me—if you have never cultivated this area of your life you are in for a wonderful experience. The rewards and benefits are unlimited and giving will make you richer in ways you never dreamed. Generosity and success go hand in hand. However, to give in order to get is simply a form of manipulation and cannot be considered a pure motive.

By developing a giving attitude you will more quickly destroy any beliefs that you are deprived and lacking; you will stop feeling that you don't have what you want and that you can't afford to be generous with others. Your feelings of self-pity will vanish. And you won't believe what will happen in your life. You will stop seeing yourself as helpless and a victim of your own situation. That which your life radiates is a clear indication of what's inside.

Every life well lived should include giving back regularly. Then that life has meaning!

When You Have Needs . . .
Remember . . .

"One man gives freely, yet gains even more; another witholds unduly, but comes to poverty. A generous man will prosper; he who refreshes others will himself be refreshed."

—The Old Testament (Proverbs 11:24–25)

CHAPTER 4

A New and Improved Quality of Life

A New Mind-set

Without a change of attitude—a new mind-set, revamping your financial life may well result in resentment and even exasperation. You can keep a spending record and follow a spending plan religiously with satisfactory results, but unless you change your outlook you will undoubtedly become a regular attender of your own pity parties.

If you say "I can't afford it" with an attitude of poverty, self-denial and anger that your life situation has put you in this terrible state of affairs, I can guarantee you will surely be miserable and a likely candidate to start debting again—sinking into a deeper mess than before. You will become a likely victim of every new credit card offering and every scam to come down the pike.

But if you consciously determine to take on a new attitude of "I can't afford it because I have chosen to save ten percent, to pay the rent, to pay my bills,

59

to give to others and to repay my debts," then you will begin to experience the serenity that accompanies financial responsibility and integrity. It is this kind of attitude that will propel you into financial recovery. The more progress you make, the greater your momentum will be, and the faster your debts will decrease. And provided you are truly committed to removing unsecured debt from your life and living according to your income, the changes will happen rapidly. Running from financial problems feels terrible, but running to financial health and economic freedom feels good. All it takes is a new attitude!

Taking Control

Reading all the books in the world, attending every workshop ever created and all the wishing imaginable will not make one wit of difference in your life unless you take control. Debt and financial gloom have controlled you long enough. It's time for action! Don't procrastinate. Don't stagnate. Maybe you need to shave only $100 off your monthly expenses to give you back financial health. Or maybe you are in a much deeper mess like I was. Wherever you are financially, make a plan and start implementing it now. Don't live one more day being victimized by your circumstances.

As you take one small step in the right direction, you will find that the next step will be easier. And then you will be able to take a medium-size step and then another and another, and then a little hop, maybe a skip and later a giant leap.

I can't begin to say that you will never again be tempted to take up debting. Even after years of recovering I am still tempted on a regular basis. We receive at least four invitations every week to accept some new credit card or line of credit. All the department stores whose credit cards I used to carry must miss me terribly. They send all kinds of temptations in the form of free gifts, discounts and glitzy customer services to convince me that I really need to return to their stores with their shiny new plastic cards in tow. It always sounds good. I have found my best defense is to read all of the fine print and spend just a moment remembering the bondage I felt when I gave into their sly invitations. Within seconds I am jerked back to reality as I calculate the usurious interest rates they try to hide, not to mention all of the other fees and charges. Just like wolves in sheeps' clothing, these offerings look real good on the surface.

No one can force you to incur debt. Nothing can make you borrow money or buy something on credit. You might go through some difficult times where you think debting is the only solution. Remain strong and committed to your plan. You will find a way out. Set your mind now—find your new attitude and don't turn back "no way, no how!"

De-junk!

Things. Possessions. Treasures. Necessities. Junk. Terms all applied to the stuff that fills our homes, garages, basements, trunks—our lives. Most of us have become quite accustomed to the process of acquiring. Funny, isn't it, how everything we manage to add to our treasure trove requires something from its owner? If it doesn't need periodic painting, it needs to be polished, mowed, scrubbed, oiled, fed, fueled, stored, filed or insured. And as more things find their way in, rarely is something of equal size or maintenance requirement banished in order to make room. Many people find that the effort of maintaining ownership greatly offsets the benefits!

Think back to when your life was the simplest. It was probably when your joy was derived from relationships, creativity and accomplishments. Slowly those qualities of life are strangled by the mountains, piles and rooms full of stuff; things which at one time were absolutely necessary but all too soon have become excess, just another form of bondage.

Too many things in your life will end up robbing you of your emotional energy and eventually your joy. Think about it. Perhaps by de-junking your home and surroundings, you will de-junk your life and actually raise your standard of living. Never underestimate the beauty of simplicity! De-junking may well be a cheap and easy way to start some meaningful action which will assist in getting your financial life in order.

Prosperity: the condition of thriving, progress and constant improvement

Abundance: a quantity that is more than enough

CHAPTER 5

Kids and Cash

Family Battleground

There are few aspects of family life that seem to offer as much potential for trouble as does money. Kids pick up attitudes from their parents—that can be good—and that can be bad. If you don't believe me, listen when your kids are playing house or talking on the phone. You'll swear you are listening to yourself! Not bad when they emulate your finest qualities. But remember, they have a great propensity for doing as you do and not as you say and if those two things don't line up, you may have trouble.

My fear that Jeremy and Josh would grow up as messed up in the money department as I was encouraged Harold and me to seriously look into the whole matter. About the time they were in elementary school I began having great discomfort over the conflict between the values we so desperately wanted to pass on to them and the way that I was abusing our financial situation. On the one hand we held honesty and integrity to be of utmost importance. Lying was absolutely not tolerated in our house. But what was I doing when I would assure the bill collectors that "the check was in the mail" (when I knew it wasn't)? Or what was I doing when I would write a check knowing full well that there were not adequate funds to cover it? While teaching my children the dangers of peer pressure, I was giving into it by needing to appear to be something I wasn't—just to be accepted by my own peers.

My desire that our children would not end up in the mess we were in helped drive us to our senses. (Isn't it amazing how our intense desire for our children's goodwill pushes us to achieve and behave in ways we previously thought impossible?) We had heard stories in past years about Harold's uncle and aunt who had reared four boys who had all become productive, respectable and financially responsible men. They had practiced what seemed to us to be some pretty unconventional methods—but they worked! And who can argue with success? We knew that if our boys modeled themselves on what they saw their parents doing they would surely be headed for financial trouble—so what did we have to lose? Of course we had to change what we were doing and at the same time design and adopt the Hunt Kid Financial Plan.

Devise a Plan

The basic premise is this: Instead of using the term *allowance,* we paid our boys a "salary." *Allowance* is a term that most children are familiar with and about which they have preconceived notions. It also carries some feeling of entitlement and more often than not it is determined according to what friends and relatives feel a child's allowance should be. We chose a term, *salary,* that was not so familiar to our boys, which we could define and create respect for. Their salary was paid monthly with the following stipulations: They had to save 10 percent and they had to give away 10 percent. Of the remaining 80 percent they alone would decide how to spend it.

Next, we taught them that everything in life is either essential or optional. The rule was that we would pay for life's essentials and the boys would pay for all optionals out of their salary as they alone decided. Of course the essentials vs. optionals changed from year to year. As the essential list shifted, designating more and more things to the optional side, the salary increased as well. The goal was that by the time the boys left home, they would be comfortable and responsible in handling all of their own finances, including buying their own clothes as well as paying for everything that happened outside of the home.

Both boys were assigned household chores commensurate with their age and ability. Their salaries, however, were not tied to, nor conditional upon, performance of those chores. The two items were separate. Failure to complete chores as assigned was dealt with and we found the most effective method was to issue a citation accompanied by a fine. Of course the fine had to be paid out of the salary and all of a sudden became a very serious matter. Very few citations were given. Needless to say, this method of discipline worked very well!

Implement the Plan

Here are some specific examples of how we implemented our plan: When Jeremy entered grade six (same plan followed for Josh two years later) he started receiving a salary ($50.00 per month). We made a specific, written list of the things he would be required to pay for such as video games, gifts for birthday parties, treats from ice cream truck, toys and school lunches (he could take lunch from home to save money). We paid for his shelter, utilities (good opportunity to teach about the cost of hot water, lights, etc.), food, clothing (we set base prices and he was required to pay for any upgrades for certain brands).

Each year, as the boys started a new school year, we reviewed the essential vs. optional list and moved more and more items over to the child's side of the ledger. The more responsibility they were given, the better they liked it. As the new salary was reviewed it was a great time to teach them that "to whom much is given, much is required."

Over the years we found it necessary to make adjustments and exceptions. For instance, we all agreed that sports and camping experiences are very important in kids' lives—and very expensive. In these cases we would determine what portion of the tuition or fee we would pay and the boys' had to plan and save the portion for which they were responsible. They still made the choice of whether or not to participate. I have to say that allowing them to make these decisions wasn't always the easiest thing, but I am glad that we didn't step in and take back control of these limited areas.

The hard part for the parents is allowing the child to make dumb financial mistakes. But that is how meaningful learning occurs. The key is to make sure that the mistakes happen on a small scale over the safety net of parental nurturing. It is important that the child determine what options he can afford. When the choice is made, the parent ceases to be the "bad guy."

As far as the saving and giving stipulations were concerned—this reflected our own personal values. We opened school savings accounts at our local bank (no fees, no minimums) and the boys made their deposits each month. They learned to fill out the deposit slip and interact with the teller. They kept their own passbooks and learned how to calculate their current balances. Our boys were given several options of charitable organizations for their savings; however, they followed our lead and gave 10 percent through our church.

Fringe Benefits

The remarkable results to date are that both of our boys saved far and beyond the 10 percent. They have each purchased a car—with cash. They pay for all of their own maintenance and gasoline. Jeremy and Josh both have become unusually financially responsible (at times putting their mother to shame). I believe that this has contributed to their own sense of self-confidence and self-reliance. We've had eight years to evaluate our plan and there is absolutely no question that it has been extremely successful.

Prior to 1984 the whole subject of money meant conflict between us and the kids. I believe that through the eyes of a child, parents have unlimited financial resources and so because of their special position in the family, *kids* feel entitled to as much of it as they can possibly finagle, wangle or otherwise manipulate. No matter how much they manage to get, it's never enough. And why shouldn't they feel that way? From birth we protect, nurture, provide for and fulfill every possible need and desire. But with each ensuing year those desires and needs change from diapers and formula to video games and compact discs. And without much notice, rhyme or reason (or so it appears to the kid) the parents cut off the flow of unlimited amounts of this nurturing (in the form of cash) and quit providing every little desire, expecting that magically the kids will understand little things like the high cost of living, inflation, skyrocketing food prices and nonexistent pay increases.

When our plan went into effect, the change literally happened overnight. Because our kids had their own money with clear areas of responsibility, they began making limited financial decisions for themselves. Within a matter of weeks a ten-year-old boy went from begging, whining and demanding to buy from the passing ice cream truck, to contemplating the high cost of this particular commodity and opting instead to not spend the quarter.

Over the last eight years we have watched our boys become very responsible with money. Passing our funds through their scrutiny has resulted in a greater portion being saved. Because they both do all of their own banking (checking and savings accounts), I believe that they have maturity in this area beyond their years. This has brought confidence and self-reliance which will undoubtedly pay off big when they are ready to leave home. The "salary" they receive is certainly not so great that they will be bound to us forever. For example, they both chose to work during the summers to supplement their salary during the lean school months. All these kinds of decisions are their own. It's great.

I am not saying that our plan would work for everyone. I do recommend, however, that you come up with some way of teaching your children to handle money—their own money. As long as they feel it's your money, no amount will ever be enough. It is a marvelous area of life where you will be able to teach about right choices and the consequences of bad ones.

The matters of borrowing, interest and debt will undoubtedly come up as children live in a world where it is "acceptable" to buy now and pay later. This is the perfect time to teach your own value system. Keep the lessons simple.

Not Bribery

When adults use money to influence the behavior of other adults, it is called bribery. Parents often use money to influence the behavior of their children and this use of bribery can result in kids doing things for the wrong reasons. Withholding a child's salary until he has completed his chores is an example of bribery. I believe it is wrong to use money for the purpose of influencing your kid's behavior— paying children to be good. The collective message will be that desired behavior requires some kind of reward.

I believe it is healthy for children to observe and to be aware of the financial struggles and decisions their parents experience. However, while I do not believe in secrecy, I don't think that children should be privy to nor carry the burdens of a past-due mortgage payment, for instance. Children do not need to be weighed down with adult-size worries. But let them see you working out your spending plan and let them know that you keep a precise spending record. Kids need to know that adults often must deny themselves certain things because there just isn't enough cash. They will learn a wonderful lesson as they observe you saving up for something you desire. Let them share your joy when you pay cash. Let them observe you giving of what you have to others. Show them solicitations you receive in the mail, the pamphlets in your bank statements, the credit card fliers next to the cash registers. These are great teaching tools. Explain that "Fly now, pay later" is a trap; "Only twelve low monthly payments" spells certain doom. Using simple figures, show them how interest can turn a bargain into a disaster.

I believe this is an area of practical living that most elementary school curricula ignore. By the time a kid reaches high school, some bad life patterns have already been established with few, if any, offsetting good patterns.

Promote Maturity

We found that teaching our kids to be financially responsible gave them a certain maturity which resulted in self-confidence and independence. While their friends are begging and manipulating their parents to part with $20.00 for the weekend, our kids are consulting their bankbook and making their own decisions. A trip to Disneyland or some other expensive activity is so much more meaningful and valuable in their eyes now. It's kind of fun to listen to them discuss the high cost of living! And often we hear "I just can't afford it," rather than "My parents won't give me the money."

The Best Preparation

No one else can prepare your kids for the future as well as you can. The child with the right outlook will have the best chance for success. Replace your children's youthful dependence with self-reliance. Instead of attempting to provide for all of their future money needs, help them understand the challenge of making money on their own. Warn them of the devastation of debt and give them a healthy and positive attitude toward money. This will prove to be a far greater and more permanent gift than giving them money itself!

CHAPTER 6

Cheap Shots

In your lifetime, you and your family in all probability will purchase an entire fleet of cars, thousands of items of clothing, tons of groceries, numerous insurance policies, drive millions of miles, repair and replace many major appliances, eat thousands of restaurant meals and help keep several utility companies in business. With a little planning and a lot of determination, there is no reason you should pay full price for any of it.

Learn to scrimp on unimportant areas of your life so you can splurge where it counts!

You can't begin too soon to reduce your expenses and improve your life. Now that you are committed to living well on 80 percent of your income it is going to be absolutely critical that you s-t-r-e-t-c-h every dollar to its absolute maximum and there's no better time than right now to get started.

Food

Never shop when hungry. Your hunger will override your good intentions every time!

Stick to a list prepared ahead of time. A little discipline never hurt anyone.

Learn to cook and bake from scratch. Get out your cookbooks and be brave. You will save a lot of money; you'll eat much better and more nutritiously and you might just enjoy it. Come on—if I can do it, anyone can!

Shop with cash. You will be a much more careful shopper knowing that if you go over your limit without a checkbook or credit card to fall back on, you will be embarrassed at the checkout.

Use coupons carefully. Very carefully! Some slick marketing program is hoping against hope that you will clip and cash in. Use coupons *only* for items you would normally buy even if you didn't have the coupon and only if it is truly a savings! Check other brands that might be on sale or are already cheaper. Manufacturers often offer coupons as incentives on new products or luxury treats. But you're not saving anything if you're suckered into it.

Have a qualified coupon? Buy smallest size allowable. You'll usually save a higher percentage of the purchase price by buying the smallest size.

Find a market that will double the coupon's value. This practice varies throughout the country, but if you do have good coupons make sure you find a way to double them. Some stores even triple them on certain days.

Shop less frequently. You will be forced to make the food last longer and you will become much more creative. Start by doubling the time between trips. If you go to the market every day, stretch it to every other day. Once a week? Shop for two weeks next time. You'll waste less, use less, and spend proportionately less.

Don't shop at convenience or specialty stores. You won't find any bargains there. Specialty items are very expensive and you can find quality substitutes at your regular or discount supermarket.

When you need to make milk and produce runs between your regular major shopping trips, make a precise list and engage the services of an errand runner (like a responsible child).

Adding a pinch of salt to milk will make it last longer.

Avoid leftovers. Your good intentions to make enough for lunch tomorrow, too, are only that— good intentions. Prepare just what you will consume. Most leftovers turn into biology specimens in the back of the fridge anyway.

Stretch fruit juice. Mix 50/50 with generic brand club soda or seltzer.

Drink water. Your doctor will love you and so will your food bill. Keep a pitcher of chilled water in the fridge. Rave about its wonderful qualities to your young children. They'll think it's a treat if you are convincing enough.

Find a thrift bakery outlet. These stores generally have very fresh products (not necessarily day-old) at cutrate prices. Shop on special 10 percent off day. Load up the freezer.

Save cookie, cake and cupcake crumbs in a plastic bag in the refrigerator and use as a topping for ice cream sundaes, fruit or muffins.

Make your own substitutes. Find recipes (send me your requests) for everything from making your own coating for chicken, pork and fish (that you shake on and bake), to sweetened condensed milk, muffin mixes, all-purpose biscuit mix and hot chocolate mix.

Eliminate choices at meals. Stick to your plan and let your family know that from now on there will be only two choices: take it or leave it.

Leave the kids home. You will stick to your shopping list with much less frustration and stress if you fly solo.

Select aisles carefully. Refuse to tread where you don't have to. Your curiosity could prove expensive!

If your market charges for grocery bags—bring your own! Recycling is a pretty good habit to get into.

Change eating habits. Learn about the nutritious benefits of beans and rice instead of meat, for example. Sneak in vegetarian meals. Experiment with legumes and grains—they are much cheaper and very good.

Come up with creative menu titles for what otherwise might be considered plain and boring: Baked

Potato Bar; Chef Salad Night; Bits and Pieces (my kids' favorite meal when they were little, thanks to Jean Frazier, the world's most loving and creative baby-sitter). Bits and Pieces is any combination of things in the fridge cut up to bite-size and cleverly arranged on a plate. Smorgasbord Night (a glorious array of this and that; you know . . . leftovers that you couldn't even think of throwing away); Hors D'oeuvres and Mocktails . . . or as my friend Emma serves now and again: Shut Up and Eat It.

Shop at a discount warehouse store. Some have annual membership fees—weigh the benefits. You'll give up the glitzy ambience but you will save big!

Learn to s-t-r-e-t-c-h. Oatmeal or bread crumbs stretch a pound of ground beef into a pound and a half or more; nonfat dry milk stretches a gallon of milk into two; borax and baking soda stretch automatic dishwashing detergent; the possibilities are endless.

Cheap gourmet coffee. Break up a cinnamon stick into dry coffee grounds or add a few drops of vanilla extract to brewed coffee.

Buy in bulk. This will cut down your trips to the grocery and will often save 50 percent of the unit cost. Reorganize your kitchen and pantry. Find places outside of kitchen to store dry and canned goods. Repackage large amounts into small units.

Use cloth napkins. Fine restaurants do. Make your own from sheets or other soft fabric. Just think of all the disposable paper products you could do without (paper plates, paper napkins, Styrofoam cups, plastic cutlery, paper towels).

Become a shelf life expert. Buying in bulk will do you no good if you end up throwing most of it away due to spoilage. Some things last indefinitely, others spoil, even if frozen, after a certain period of time.

Consider generic and store brands. Some generic items are awful and others are exactly the same product as the name brand. Do some experimenting, especially if your store offers "satisfaction guaranteed!" If you don't like it they may let you exchange it.

Make eating at home fun. Rearrange your eating area. Make a new tablecloth. Haul out some place mats. Install a ceiling fan. Light some candles.

Buy largest quantity rather than individual portions. Take soda pop for instance—cans usually cost more than bottles for some unknown reason (unless you are using a coupon in which case you have already learned to buy the smallest size allowable).

Shop the perimeter of supermarket. That is where you will typically find the produce, meat and dairy. The center aisles are the prepackaged and preprocessed high-priced items, a.k.a. the danger zone.

Plant a garden. Consider the square foot method (see your library for a how-to book) or container gardening. You don't need major acreage to grow tomatoes, herbs and an occasional row of lettuce. Gradually work up to more exotic things like carrots and beans.

Keep a price book. Start keeping a notebook which lists the prices of regularly purchased items at various stores. Keep it with you so that as you see specials or ads, you'll be able to determine whether it is really a bargain or not.

Check the reduced and day-old sections of the store. And check the expiration dates, too. No buy is a good buy if you have to throw it out.

Avoid shopping on the first of the month. Some stores have been known to raise their prices during the time welfare and Social Security checks come out.

Shop late in the day. Ask the butcher or produce person if there is anything they will be marking down. You'll be surprised how helpful they can be and you'll get the best of the sale items.

Don't shop when you are exhausted. You will not be as disciplined or effective.

Watch for refunds and rebates. Be careful—your time is precious but if you can fit it in, there's money to be made.

Make your own pizza stone! This is the key to professional quality pizza. Instead of paying $30.00 for commercial pizza stone, pick up an unglazed terra-cotta tile at your local hardware for about a buck. Place on lowest rack in oven, heat up to 400 degrees and bake pizza directly on tile.

Make your own salad dressings and croutons. You will save at least 50 percent. We have some terrific recipes!

Always use powdered dry milk in baking. If recipe

calls for cream or condensed milk, use only half the usual amount of water you would use with the dry milk.

Paper coffee filters can be used several times. Just carefully rinse them off between usings.

Reserve eating out for special occasions. Restaurant and fast food will cost you at least double. Consider eating out an occasional treat.

Weigh all produce, even if it is priced per item. You won't believe the difference in weight of the prebagged carrots, for instance! Even with a weight printed on the bag, the real weight may be quite different. Heads of lettuce priced individually can differ in weight by as much as half a pound! Get the most for your money.

Buy produce in a bag for the best value. Watch out—often the bruised and spoiled fruit will find its way into the bottom of a bag. Just pick out the best bag!

Load up on loss leaders. These are the advertised sale items that the store uses as bait to get you in the door. Buy as much as you can reasonably use—no more and nothing else!

Store cartons of cottage cheese and sour cream upside down in fridge. They will keep twice as long.

Cooking in cast iron pots boosts the iron content of food. Soup simmered for a few hours in an iron pot has almost thirty times more iron than soup cooked in another pan. Health is important in keeping down medical expenses!

To keep fish fresh and odorless rinse with fresh

lemon juice and water, dry thoroughly, wrap and refrigerate.

Make your own baby food. Check your library or bookstore for a how-to book. Freeze in ice cube trays to make convenient individual servings.

Clean out and rearrange pantry often. Check for expiration dates. You won't believe the neat stuff you'll find that you forgot you had.

Frozen orange juice concentrate is typically cheaper than ready-to-drink. It lasts longer, too.

Consider a vacuum sealing machine. It won't save you money if you don't use it, though. Makes buying in bulk a much more sensible activity.

Get a freezer. Too expensive? Consider sharing space with a neighbor or friend.

A full freezer is an efficient freezer. If you don't have enough food to keep it jam-packed, fill plastic jugs (leave room for expansion) with water and freeze. You'll have fresh water in case of a power failure and the frozen jugs will keep the freezer contents cold much longer.

Don't wash. Berries will freeze better if they aren't washed first. Any other washed fruit must be thoroughly dried before freezing.

Freeze strawberries whole. Remove leaves but leave stems.

Zip-type plastic bags make great freezer containers. Squeeze out as much air as possible before zipping closed.

Keep a written index of freezer contents. Hang in handy location. This way you can spend as much time as you need looking through inventory to make a decision without having the door open, letting in hot air.

Freezing should happen quickly. When putting things in the freezer, spread them out so all sides are in contact with the cold. When frozen, move everything together compactly.

Do not refreeze thawed food. I don't know why. It has something to do with enzymes and spoilage.

Vegetables must be blanched before freezing. They contain enzymes which, if their action is not stopped, will cause the product to become coarse and flavorless. Enzymes defy freezing but cannot withstand heat. Before freezing, drop fresh vegetables into boiling water and transfer immediately into ice water. Work with small batches.

Freeze onions. Chop, spread out in one layer on cookie sheet. Place quickly in coldest place in freezer. When frozen, transfer to bag or container.

Freeze mushrooms. Do not wash. Clean with bristle brush. Chop and freeze in same manner as onions.

Proper wrapping is key to successful freezing. Materials must be waterproof and moisture and vapor resistant to prevent food from drying out. Wrap very tightly, removing as much air as possible. Seal with tape.

Freeze brown and powdered sugars. Prevents lumps.

Freeze coffee. Either beans or ground. Maintains freshness.

Freeze nuts. Retards spoilage. Nuts left in pantry will become rancid.

Freeze popcorn kernels. Will stay fresh forever and will encourage every kernel to pop!

Freeze marshmallows, potato chips, pretzels, crackers and popcorn. Works best if frozen in original unopened containers.

Never freeze mayonnaise, boiled potatoes, meringues and custards. I don't know why. Just trust me and don't waste your time or money.

Clothing

Paying retail is stupid. With so many manufacturer outlets, discount mail-order catalogs and fantastic sales, you should never pay full sticker price!

Buy fewer but buy classic. Rethink your wardrobe to include fewer pieces. Make those few pieces classic items which look great year in and year out. Stay away from trends or fads.

Coordinate. Stick to a basic color scheme so you can mix and match to create more outfits with what you have.

Accessorize. Well-chosen accessories can turn the same basic dress or suit into four or five different looks.

Find a good alterations person. A good tailor can take in, let out, take up, let down and redesign a classic and well-made garment.

Avoid "dry clean only." This kind of expensive

maintenance will double or even triple the cost of a garment.

If you must, find a good, reasonable dry cleaner. There are cleaners who charge a flat rate ($1.50 per item). Shop carefully.

Repair, resole, reheel. A good shoe repair can do miracles for your shoes. You can easily double or triple the life of a good pair of shoes. Also a good place to have luggage, handbags and belts repaired.

Recycle. Instead of having your children wear their siblings' hand-me-downs, trade with neighbors or friends who have children of the same sizes. The kids get a new look and the price is right.

Leave your good business shoes at the office. Change into an older pair when leaving to tromp up and down steps and out to the parking lot.

Consignment shop. A very fashionable wave of the nineties is the consignment shop! High quality previously owned clothes are sold at often 70–85 percent of the new price. Shop well and you will find unbelievable bargains. Shhhhhh! It's your secret.

Wash with cold water. Unless you are dealing with unusual stains, cold water and good detergent will clean just as well as warm or hot water. You'll save on hot water, the fabrics will last longer and colors will stay bright much longer.

Thrift shops. Be careful—frumpiness is not allowed. But if you have the time you might be able to save a lot of money there. Never buy just because it's a good bargain.

Change your clothes. As soon as you get home

from work, change out of your expensive business suit into casual clothing to minimize the chance of stains and snags.

Rent rather than buy. Especially good tip for formal wear including evening gowns, mother-of-the-bride and bridal gowns. Shop around. Tuxedo rental prices vary tremendously.

Stock up off season. Especially if you have a crystal ball to tell you how much your kids will grow in a year! Seasonal items (swim wear, coats, boots, etc.) are often cleared out at phenomenal prices, so if you can handle the thought of buying snow wear in the spring—go for it!

Borrow maternity clothes. Start a co-op with your friends. Typically, maternity clothes don't get that much wear and are easy to maintain.

Become a stain guru. Removing an ugly stain may allow another year of wear.

Use shampoo on collar and cuff rings. Shampoo is meant to clean body oil, which is what that ring around the collar and cuffs is. Baby shampoo is an excellent substitute for expensive cold water soap.

Sew buttons once and for all. Use dental floss for thread.

Avoid shopping at the last minute. Start planning ahead for your clothing needs. Last minute stress is costly.

Buy men's white T-shirts to wear under jackets, ladies. They're cheap, easy to dye or trim and are machine washable.

As a general rule, stay away from leather, suede and silk. They are lovely but expensive to maintain.

Hand wash delicates. Take them into the shower with you—and use your shampoo on them.

Household

De-junk your home. If you are like most people, you have about twice as much stuff as you really like, use or need. Have nothing in your home that you do not know to be useful or believe to be beautiful.

Learn to make repairs. Very few household repairs are dangerous. Read manuals, take classes, be brave and tackle those things that are not going to endanger your well-being. Look for *How to Do Just About Anything* (Reader's Digest Association).

Measure detergent for both washing machine and dishwasher. If you use the dump method you are probably using way too much.

Recycle. Find new uses for things that are about to exceed their normal lifespan. For instance, worn-out bath towels make terrific car washing rags. Worn-out socks and diapers make good dusters.

Shaving cream is one of the most effective upholstery cleaners.

Buy queen-size top sheets for king-size beds. King-size top sheets are usually way too big and require major tucking in. A queen-size flat works great on most king-size beds—and is a lot cheaper.

Buy sheets instead of yardage. Buying sheets on sale gives you extra wide yardage at a mere fraction of the cost of yard goods. Perfect for making curtains, tablecloths, napkins, pillows, nightclothes and crafts.

Instead of buying finished area rugs buy a remnant from a carpet store and have it bound. Usually much cheaper.

Arrange for regular monthly bills to be paid directly out of your account by your bank. You'll save the costs of postage, late fees, checks and envelopes.

Save receipts, warranties and owner's manuals. Often these are all you will need to have an appliance repaired at no charge. Find a nifty binder that will keep everything neat and orderly.

Fire the maid. Get all the occupants of the house involved in cleaning. Learn speed-cleaning techniques.

Buy unfinished furniture. A little practice will go a long way and usually the store will give you a quick lesson. Buy the finishing products from a discount hardware store.

Beware of home shopping by television. The products are highly overpriced, overrated and pitched to the compulsive shopper.

Learn to shop without buying. Just a little change of attitude will allow you to thoroughly enjoy lovely things but leave them in the stores. Let someone else dust, polish and care for them. You can visit ''your stuff'' whenever you like and change your mind without consequence!

Get friendly with salespeople. They usually know

when things are going to go on sale. Ask and then be willing to wait.

Rent carpet cleaning equipment. Save big time by doing this chore yourself. You can usually rent better equipment than you could afford to own.

Clean the garage or basement. Hold a sale and get rid of what you don't use so you can organize what you do.

Read magazines and books to learn cheap home decorating tricks. Picture framing, using sheets to make curtains and pillows, stenciling, wallpapering are easy and fun, too. Look for these materials at the library. They're *free!*

Make your own cleaning products. No more high-priced commercial products.

Make dust cloths by dipping cheesecloth into a mixture of 2 cups water and $1/4$ cup lemon oil. Let dry.

Clean silk flowers. Pop them into a paper bag with a small handful of uncooked rice. Shake to remove dust. Throw rice out—who knows what was hiding in those flowers.

No need to clean paint roller covers and brushes until your job is completely finished. Just wrap them tightly in plastic wrap overnight (or a couple of days) and keep them in the freezer. They'll stay soft and usable until you're ready to finish.

Store partially full cans of paint upside down. The paint will form an airtight seal, extending the useful life.

Oil stains on driveway. To remove ugly oil stains,

sprinkle with kitty litter and "scrub" with a brick. Repeat for stubborn stains.

Household deodorizer. Put a cinnamon stick or a few whole cloves in vacuum cleaner bag to make your house smell clean and fresh. (Doesn't work unless you actually run the vacuum!)

Remove ink marks from plastic. Spray with hair spray and wipe clean.

Sharpen scissors. Cut through a piece of 220 grit sandpaper.

Utilities

Buy energy efficient. When selecting a new appliance look for the yellow tag with the "EER" on it. The higher the number the less wasteful of energy and more efficient it is.

Preheat oven only if the recipe tells you to. Casseroles and roasts don't suffer from starting out cold.

Let your fingers do the walking even if it requires a toll call; it's cheaper than driving your car.

Check to see if you have deposits on account. Usually if you have been a good customer (gas, water, electricity, phone) for at least a year, you can arrange to have your deposits refunded or credited toward your account. You should be able to get interest, too—if you ask.

If someone in your family has a vision impairment you may be able to get free directory assistance.

Take short showers instead of water guzzling baths.

Install a flow controlling shower head. Your kids will never notice, but your water bill will.

If your phone service is interrupted for more than 24 hours ask for a credit. You'll probably get it, especially if you nicely point out that you pay dearly for the privilege of having a telephonic link to the outside world.

Always check for a toll free number before dialing long distance; 800 Directory Assistance is free (1-800-555-1212).

Close off seldom-used rooms so that you don't have to heat them in cold weather or cool them during the hot months.

Put up storm windows and add weather stripping around doors and windows. Anything you can do to make your home airtight will reduce your heating/cooling bills.

Conserve electricity by using a carpet sweeper (one of those push-type gizmos with brush rollers) instead of vacuuming every day. Vacuuming once a week will probably be more than sufficient for deep cleaning.

Substitute a fluffy comforter for your electricity sucking electric blanket.

Put an egg timer by the phone to remind you to hang up before you talk yourself into debt oblivion.

Call corporate collect. Try it. Most large companies will accept your collect call as a matter of course. Just identify yourself as a good customer or potential client. If denied—just call back direct. Hey, it's worth a try and usually works.

Always ask for credit immediately upon dialing a wrong number. Don't be embarrassed. It's routine.

Have a phone checkup annually. Request an equipment inventory report. The phone company will send you a form listing the services for which you are charged. If you find you've been overpaying, demand a retroactive refund.

Consider having telephone company block 900 numbers. They are never free and can cost as much as $20 a minute.

Turn off oven or stove right before an item is completely finished. Whatever heat is left in the oven is usually enough to finish the job.

Use glass or ceramic. If you use these baking dishes in the oven you can lower heat by up to 25 degrees than called for by recipe.

Burner should equal pan size. Pan should completely cover burner to avoid energy waste.

Three-way bulbs are more efficient provided you use the lower wattage whenever possible. Dimmer switches are good energy conservers as well.

Don't open fridge or freezer until you are sure what you are going after.

Instead of leaving coffeepot warming for hours on end, transfer finished coffee to a thermos and turn that energy sucker off.

Replace cracked or loose gasket around refrigerator door.

Run only full dishwasher. Otherwise you are wasting precious hot water and electricity.

Keep hot water heater at about 120 degrees

(midrange). Water will wash just as efficiently and will be less apt to scald.

Run dishwasher in the evening and turn off before dry cycle. Open door and allow dishes to air dry overnight.

Wrap blanket type insulation around hot water heater. Savings over the first year will probably more than pay for the blanket.

Draw drapes or close awnings to cut down on heating and air-conditioning. They act as great insulators.

Check weather stripping around windows and doors annually. Replace if necessary.

Insulate your basement to prevent loss of heat and cool. The cost should be recouped within three years.

Many utility companies will visit your home and give you free advice on how you can conserve energy better.

Fabric wall hangings like a quilt or decorative rug will insulate interior walls and keep your room cozier with the thermostat turned down.

If you leave a room for more than 15 minutes, turn off the lights.

Stove or range top uses less energy than your oven. Cook topside whenever possible.

Smaller appliances such as electric skillets or woks, and slow-cookers and pressure cookers use less energy than a range or oven.

Set refrigerator thermostat at 38 to 40 degrees F. This is probably about 10 degrees lower than recommended by manufacturer, but can cut running costs by almost 25 percent. To get similar savings from freezer set it between 0 and 5 degrees F.

Vacuum the coils at the bottom or back of your refrigerator frequently to prevent dust from building up around them. Dust makes the refrigerator run more often and so does keeping it too close to the wall. The refrigerator and freezer need room to breathe or else they get too hot and run too much.

Make sure to turn off curling iron, clothes iron, lights, coffeepot, etc., when not in use.

When baking keep track of cooking time with a timer. Don't keep peeking into oven. Each peek can cost as much as 25 degrees F; it can also affect browning and baking.

Install timers and/or motion detectors rather than leaving lights on all night. This will ensure you're using lights only when necessary.

Fill a small plastic bottle with water. Place it in your toilet tank away from the flushing mechanism. Its displacement will make the water volume requirement less and your toilet will still flush just fine.

Buy your own phone. Renting from the phone company is very expensive.

Consider energy efficient light bulbs. They cost more up front but you will save a lot over the long term.

Make sure your light bulbs are the correct wattage for the appliance. Putting a 150 watt bulb in a 75 watt socket is not only wasting energy—it could cause a fire.

Reacquaint yourself with a clothesline. Hanging out a few loads of laundry each week instead of using a gas or electric clothes dryer can save hundreds of dollars each year.

Turn off water heater when away on vacation.

Install water saving toilets when you need to replace. Check with your utility company. Many offer rebates in excess of the cost of a new commode just for your trouble.

Check for leaks. Drop a little food coloring into the toilet tank. Observe if any color shows up in the bowl. If so, you have a leak! Fix it.

Water your lawn at night. Sunshine encourages evaporation. By watering at night, more water will stay on the lawn and penetrate into the roots, allowing your watering time to be shorter than during daylight hours.

Close fireplace damper unless you have a fire going.

Check out your phone bill. Phone companies are not perfect and chances are you've been paying for someone else's phone calls.

Call during cheapest hours. Usually nights and weekends.

Avoid directory assistance. I can't believe they actually charge for that, but they do. Get a phone book.

Use $.19 postcards to communicate on nonurgent matters. Much cheaper than a long-distance phone call.

Put your phone service on "vacation" while you are out of town. The savings are modest but every little bit helps.

Reconsider all the phone add-ons. Maybe you aren't even using some of the features you're paying for (call waiting, call forwarding, speed dialing, etc.).

Buy heating oil off season. Start checking prices in the spring. Typically you should be able to take advantage of lowest prices from July to September.

Freeze before you freeze. This only works if you live in a cold climate. Putting room temperature items in your refrigerator or freezer actually heats up the environment in there for a while. During the winter months put these items outdoors to cool before going into fridge or freezer.

Insurance

Take higher deductibles. In essence you partially self-insure by being willing to take the chance that you won't get sick or you won't crash the car or you won't get burglarized. The higher the deductible, the lower the premium. The insurance company actually compensates the customer who is willing to share a greater portion of the risk.

Commute by car pool. Most insurance companies offer discounts to low-mileage drivers.

Stay out of the death lane. The far left lane is where speeders hang out and most accidents occur.

Drive for five drivers. Yourself, drivers in front, both sides and behind you. Be prepared for them to do the unexpected.

Have adequate protection. With the higher deductibles you can afford better coverage, which is a wise move.

Find a company that gives discounts for having all of your different insurance with the same company. Insurance companies *can* offer volume discounts.

Call your agent every year to make sure all their information is correct and that they are aware of your teenage son's good driving record and three years' experience. All of those things might matter.

Install timers on a radio as well as on outdoor and indoor lights. They are cheap protection. Burglars tend to avoid a home if they think there's a chance someone's there.

Don't be predictable. A car that's always parked in the same place for the same amount of time each day or night lets thieves know where to look for it and how much time they'd need to make off with it.

Ask about discounts for security systems, smoke alarms, good driving records, etc. Always ask! The agent or company may not volunteer.

Add replacement-cost rider to renter or home-owner insurance. May cost a little more, but in case of a claim you will be glad you did. Without it, the company will depreciate the value of every item and you will be a big loser.

Consider umbrella liability. It is very cheap and could be a lifesaver, especially if you have kids and your exposure is great. Check with your agent.

Don't make small claims. Too many can lead to policy cancellations or premium hikes. Insurance companies think that a frequent filer is heading for a serious accident.

File for diminution of value against the other guy's insurance company if the damage to your car was the other guy's fault. Even though it is repaired adequately, you have a diminished resale value for which you should be compensated. On average you can file for 10 percent of the total repair cost! Be persistent.

Don't buy travel insurance. It's one of the biggest rip-offs.

If possible, pay premiums annually. Avoid the added costs for monthly or quarterly billing.

Don't put insurance policies in a safe deposit vault. These boxes are often sealed by court order when the box holder dies. Could cause a substantial delay.

Do single persons need life insurance? Only if someone is financially dependent on you.

Scrutinize your deck sheet every renewal. This is the coverage sheet that shows your limits. Don't overinsure. Computers have a way of sneaking stuff in.

Make sure you are with a highly rated company. These days the smaller, lower-rated companies are dropping out regularly. Better safe than sorry.

Buy term life insurance. Experts that I trust advise that whole life or universal life are not wise investments. Check with your own professional—but check.

Don't buy life insurance for kids. Makes absolutely no sense. Insure only wage earners (including stay home moms!) whose untimely departure would create a financial hardship.

Don't buy too much life insurance. Make sure it is adequate to maintain current life-styles and needs. Don't let your agent decide how much you need. He wants to make a big sale! You decide. Insurance companies will say that a family needs at least enough life insurance to cover four or five times its yearly income.

Cut back on life insurance as your dependents become independent. Providing for a spouse alone takes less than a spouse and eight kids!

Never buy insurance from television or direct-mail ads. This is a sleazy marketing ploy. The premiums are at least 400 percent too high for the coverage and the exclusions are mammoth.

Drop your comprehensive and collision insurance when the value of your car drops below $2,000. Save the difference in premiums to buy another car.

Videotape your home inside and out for insurance records. In case of a fire you need to have evidence of the expensive wall coverings and decorator window coverings. While you are taping, narrate aloud and describe in detail. Keep tape in safe deposit box. Make sure video date is well documented. Revideo every few years or when considerable changes are made. Tapes don't last forever, either.

If you rent, buy a tenant's policy. This is a must. Landlords are not responsible for your belongings in case of disaster.

Never buy credit disability insurance, automobile service contracts, extended warranties on appliances and electronics, or Chargegard (for credit cards).

Never buy mortgage life insurance. This is the kind of policy tied to your mortgage or other credit purchase which will pay off the balance in case of your death. If you think you need the additional insurance arrange it yourself and leave your heirs the choice of paying off the mortgage or not.

Transportation

Think long and hard before buying new. Since financing charges are so great, paying cash is the method of choice, and new cars are expensive.

Research. Check *Consumer Reports* and other publications to learn all you can before making a decision.

February is the best month to buy. The second best time is two weeks before Christmas. Terrible weather provides a good time to make a deal.

Choose a car not coveted by criminals. In 1991 the five most frequently stolen cars were the '85, '86 and '87 Chevrolet Camaro and the '84 and '85 Oldsmobile Cutlass Supreme.

Don't carry more than you need. A light load gets much better gas mileage. Clean out heavy items from trunk. Don't make your car a mobile warehouse for stuff you can leave in the garage.

Avoid roof and trunk racks. These things ruin aerodynamics and cut down gas mileage.

Never drive when angry or upset. Angry drivers waste fuel, are dangerous to themselves and others on the road and are hard on the engine.

Listen to traffic reports to avoid tie-ups and congestion. You may be able to change routes and avoid costly congestion.

A thirty-second warm-up is sufficient for modern day cars. Any longer and you are just wasting precious fuel.

Be gentle and keep it steady. A light foot on the accelerator will certainly save fuel.

Slow down. Not only will you get optimum performance, you may avoid a costly ticket and unfortunate insurance increases.

Regular scheduled maintenance pays off every day. It makes parts last longer, prevents most emergency breakdowns and promotes good gas mileage.

Be observant: Look, listen and sniff occasionally for anything unusual about your car. You know your car best and early diagnosis will pay off later. Take note of odd noises, hard starting or significant loss of power.

Have your brakes replaced before the rotors have

to be turned. You'll save hundreds of dollars. Your mechanic should check for free and tell you how much of the pad is remaining. Don't push it past 5 percent.

Check your own fluid levels. Just a little time and patience will go a long way to keep engine, brakes and transmission in tip-top shape. Make sure you have a reliable teacher.

Learn how to do some of your regular maintenance. Books, videotapes, colleges, adult schools all can teach you about routine maintenance. It's not so hard to fix a car—the hard part is figuring out what's wrong!

Find a professional you can trust to handle the major stuff. Don't be afraid to get a second opinion.

Corroded battery terminals can leave you stranded. Quick fix: Pour a cola drink or other carbonated beverage over terminals. It will act like baking soda to eat through the corrosion. This is a temporary measure to get you where you need to go without a tow.

Keep tires inflated properly. Underinflated will drag down gas mileage—overinflated will cause premature wear.

Buy the smallest car you can live with. Weight is the biggest enemy of fuel economy.

Keep your cars longer. Proper maintenance will allow you to keep a car for ten years or longer. My professional insists that if maintained right, a car should serve faithfully for over 300,000 miles.

Use public transportation whenever possible. It's

still cheaper than driving your own—especially if you are alone.

Rent. If you live in a big city with good public transportation, sell your car and rent one on the rare occasion that you really need it. You'll save on insurance, wear and tear, not to mention parking.

Sell an extra car. Do you really need two, three, or four cars?

Pay cash for used. Makes much better sense than financing a new auto. Auto loans carry huge interest rates.

Skip the vanity license plates. Find a cheaper way to promote yourself.

Buy at end of the month. Take advantage of lagging quotas.

Check on insurance rates before you make a decision. Call your agent with a couple of choices and get quotes.

Avoid fancy options. They just mean that there are many more expensive things to go wrong.

Yellow rear turn signals. Research suggests that cars with yellow turn signals are less likely to be hit from behind while turning than cars with red signals.

Never agree to buy dealer's options. Extended warranties, fancy paint job protectors, racing stripes, sunroof—these are huge profit items for the dealer.

Leasing only encourages trading in more often. Even the best lease is going to cost you more in the long run.

Sell your old car yourself. The dealer will probably never give you what you can get yourself.

Looking to buy a particular previously owned car? This is great. Call 1-800-CAR SEARCH. This is an absolutely free national service that will search for your car of choice, while you wait.

Need to sell? Call 1-800-CAR SEARCH. They'll match you up with a buyer and charge $14.95 per month to your phone bill. That beats any other kind of advertising I know of.

Drive with the windows closed. Open windows mess up aerodynamics and will cost you more in gas mileage than running the air conditioner.

Pump your own gas. Full serve is outrageously more expensive. Keep a box of disposable plastic gloves handy so you don't smell like a service station attendant all day.

Inspect your fan belts. Carry a spare or two in your trunk.

Wash and wax your car yourself or teach your kids how to. Professional car washes are very expensive.

Buy oil and other fluids in bulk at the discount store. Buying oil a quart at a time at the service station is not smart.

Pay registration renewals on time. Most states hand out heavy penalties even if you are only one day late.

If you rent a car, reject offers of additional optional coverage. Be prepared for some heavy-handed tactics to get you to accept it. Salespersons get hefty bonuses if you can be persuaded.

Homeowners and Renters

Have an extra room? Consider taking in a boarder to help defray your costs. Post a notice (for free) at a local community college or corporation. Check with personnel offices at larger corporations in your area. Often they assist employees in locating affordable housing.

Get more than one bid for major repairs or improvements.

Don't fall for scams. They usually come in the form of door-to-door salespersons.

Don't overbuild the neighborhood. Usually the most expensive house in the neighborhood appreciates the least.

Location is the most important criteria in selecting a home.

Drive a hard bargain when you purchase a home. Get help from friends or relatives who are less emotionally involved.

Negotiate the closing costs. Always ask for more than you are willing to accept.

Make sure you earn interest on your deposit during escrow period.

Never allow seller to select inspectors. You want an impartial assessment of termite damage, roof condition, plumbing and electrical situations.

Make sure escrow holder is truly impartial. Often the seller's broker will steer the escrow to a company in which they have some financial interest. It is better to have an escrow with no ties.

Have your head examined before you attempt to build your own home. Unless you are a developer or professional contractor you are in for a big surprise, not the least of which is that it will cost twice what you estimate.

Change smoke detector batteries on your birthday. Also vacuum the detector to get dust and dirt out of sensors. Smoke detectors don't last forever, so make sure you test yours often and replace it readily.

Move into a smaller house. The lower costs could drastically improve your financial situation.

Use students and other nonprofessionals for odd jobs such as moving furniture, gardening, painting, carpentry and any other jobs that you cannot do yourself. Call your local college or university and ask for the job placement office.

Put cut flowers in refrigerator when you're at work, asleep, or otherwise unable to enjoy them. They'll last longer, especially if you trim the stems and freshen the water every day or so.

Ask your dry cleaner or neighborhood repair shops to let you know when they have unclaimed goods for sale. There are terrific bargains to be had.

Request a discount whenever you pay cash in a store that honors standard bank credit cards. Since they have to pay from 3 to 7 percent of the bill to the card company on a credit purchase, they should be willing to give you at least part of the difference in the form of a discount. It won't always work, but it's worth a try.

Sell by owner. Prepare for lots of aggravation and

allow time to research and learn how. You can save significant dollars.

Shop your mortgage. Programs vary a great deal. Get many opinions.

Refinance your existing mortgage. If you plan to stay in this house for the next two to three years and you can beat your present interest rate by $1^1/_2$ percent it may be a good idea. Consider the points on the new loan. Try to negotiate the closing costs and points if possible.

Pay more than the monthly payment. This is probably one of the best things you can do with extra cash. You will pay down the principal more quickly, which will result in a tremendous saving of interest.

Instead of paying your mortgage monthly, pay half of your mortgage payment every two weeks. You will end up making 26 half-payments which equals 13 monthly payments. Your spending plan will absorb this additional payment with little pain if any, and your principal will love you.

Do your own painting and decorating. Check out home improvement centers to learn the latest techniques.

If you are going to sell your home at a loss, try and hold off a while, rent it out so that you can take advantage of the tax loss when you eventually sell. Check with your accountant, but if you can show it as an investment rather than personal residence you might be able to recoup some of the loss.

Challenge your property tax bill. If your value has

declined, you might be entitled to a reassessment of your taxes.

Clean out gutters. A little tricky on a two-story home. You may, though, prevent some drainage problems in the future.

Remember your one-time $125,000 exclusion on capital gains if you are 55 or older.

Check with your city. Sometimes very low interest or grant money is available for modernizing or fixing up the outside. Be the first in line.

If you have a home business, a portion of your mortgage and related expenses may be taken as a tax deduction. It's tricky so get professional advice.

Install automatic timers on your sprinkler systems. Water less often for a longer period of time to allow deep penetration.

If you rent, find an area with rent control. If the law is in place, you might as well take advantage of it.

Get a roommate so you can afford a nicer, bigger place. Make sure the details of your agreement about who pays for what are in writing.

Negotiate the rent. In a market where many vacancies exist, the tenant is king.

Be very clear about your rental agreement before you sign anything. Deposits should be clearly spelled out. Ask for interest to be paid on deposits.

Take good care of the rental. Do not paint or wallpaper without written approval. Follow the rules and go the extra mile. You might avoid a rental hike.

Before you vacate, take extra pains to clean. No

one wants a hassle over return of deposits. The landlord will give you a good recommendation in the future and that is valuable.

Health and Personal Care

Get your hair cut, colored or curled at a beauty school. Students are usually carefully supervised, conscientious and anxious to please. Be nice but firm about your expectations and desires. Prices are unbelievably low.

Take advantage of store testers and free samples. These are often cheerfully available at cosmetic counters. Buying before trying is a waste.

Use plain talcum instead of expensive perfumed bath powder.

Stand nearly empty bottles of hand lotion, moisturizer and other creamy stuff on end for a while. The cap will accumulate enough to last another week or so.

Learn to cut your kids' hair. Learn well from someone who is good at it. You'll save at least $75.00 a year per kid.

Don't get sick. Practice preventive health maintenance now. Even with the best insurance you are going to end up paying for deductibles, copayments and prescriptions.

Never be without health insurance. High deductibles are fine because you intend to stay healthy. But one catastrophic illness or accident could wipe out everything you have saved and planned for.

Brush and floss daily. Preventive dental care is easy to practice. You can avoid costly gum disease, bridges and dentures by simply brushing, flossing and rinsing often.

Keep kids' immunizations up-to-date. Sick kids mean parents must miss work or pay for expensive alternative day care. The costs really add up. Most can be prevented.

Look for free or cheap immunization programs through your local health department.

Make great flexible ice packs: Pour $3/4$ cup water and $1/4$ cup rubbing alcohol into a zip type plastic bag and close. Put zipped bag into another bag, close up and freeze. You will have a slushy bag of ice whenever needed for sprains, headaches or whatever.

Shop health insurance coverage. Often the first year premium is much less so changing is not a bad idea. If your employer offers a menu of coverages, check them all carefully. A health maintenance organization (HMO) might be best for your particular situation.

Always get a second opinion for any major medical procedure. Doctors are human you know.

Carefully examine hospital bills. If you went in for a knee reconstruction and were billed for infant nursery time, put up a fuss. Hospitals are notorious for making these kinds of mistakes.

Find a walk-in clinic for emergencies. These 24-hour clinics are popping up all over and are much cheaper than the emergency room at a hospital.

Take your own stuff to the hospital. If your doctor approves you can arrange to take your own food, prescriptions (have doctor write these out ahead of time so you can pick them up at your discount pharmacy), TV, cellular phone (rent one) and toiletry items. Insist on an a la carte plan so you pay the absolute bare minimum. It's still going to cost a lot to be hospitalized.

If you have to be admitted to a hospital insist that you go in the day of the surgery. An early admittance will run up your bill and is usually for the convenience of the staff, not the patient.

Inquire about specific hospital fees before you are admitted. Fees do vary considerably from one hospital to the next. Why pay for the availability of kidney machines and heart transplant teams if you are having knee reconstruction?

Seventy-five percent of all antibiotics taken each year are unnecessary. Doctors know that patients who take the time and trouble to make an office visit *expect* to be "rewarded" with a prescription! Doctors like to keep their patients happy, too. Ask the prescribing doctor exactly what the prescription can and cannot do for you and if it is necessary for full recovery.

Always consider generic. Ask your doctor to prescribe the cheapest form of medicine.

Shop prescriptions. I have found that pharmacies will quote prices over the phone. Call around. You won't believe how the prices vary.

Ask doctor for free samples. Pharmaceutical com-

panies flood doctors with samples of all kinds of expensive prescriptions. If your doctor doesn't offer—
ask!

Buy routine prescriptions through the mail. There are many mail-order pharmacies that fulfill prescriptions on a 48-hour basis.

Keep track of parking fees and mileage associated with medical care for tax purposes.

Milk of magnesia makes a very cheap and effective facial masque.

Baking soda mixed with a little water is a great facial scrub.

Spritz feet and inside of shoes with rubbing alcohol in a spray type bottle. Very refreshing and eliminates foot odor!

Nail polish will last much longer if you soak your fingertips in a 50/50 mixture of warm water and white vinegar before applying it.

Try applying a wet, black tea bag to a nasty canker sore. The tannin acts as an astringent and will relieve the pain and promote healing.

Adding four tablespoons of plain yogurt to your diet each day is effective in preventing canker sores.

Don't smoke. Even an average smoking habit will cost around $1,000 a year and who knows how much more in additional health care.

Take vitamins. Especially vitamin C, which has been proven to have tremendous effects on staving off colds and flu, lowering cholesterol, decreasing arthritis pain, reducing outbreaks of canker sores, lessening premenstrual syndrome just to name a few! Staying healthy may eliminate expensive doctor visits.

Buy a book on home remedies. Make sure it is written by competent doctors and then memorize it! (*The Doctor's Book of Home Remedies* [Rodale Press] is a great one, I've found.)

Cheap hot water bottle. Fill a two-liter plastic soda pop bottle about four inches from top with hot tap water. Replace screw-top tightly. Wrap in terry cloth towel and snuggle up.

Don't throw away those empty tissue boxes. They make wonderful caddies for the car. They are the perfect size to hold sunglasses, lotion, spare change and cassette tapes and can be used for a trash receptacle in the car. They are also good storage boxes for crayons, doll clothes and puzzle pieces.

Kids and Families

Don't get divorced. A divorce most certainly will have a damaging effect on your finances, to say nothing of your emotions. Just imagine the problem of running two households on what it is taking to support one now.

Don't lend money to a friend. It's just too risky to your financial health and your friendship.

Don't lend money to family members. There is no such thing as a loan within a family. Consider it a gift and if you just happen to get paid back—it's a bonus.

Open school savings accounts for your kids. Teach

them how to fill out deposit slips and make their own deposits. These accounts usually have no minimum balances or service fees.

Share baby-sitting. Work out a plan with your friends to trade favors. Consider starting a baby-sitting co-op. Do research on others that have been successful.

Teach kids to make lunches. Brown bagging it is a good idea—even for mom and dad.

Reacquaint your family with the local public library. Current newspapers, magazines, children's books, adult books, videos, CDs, wonderful storytelling librarians—what a fabulous place the library is. And it's *free*. If you like to shop for fun, satisfy the impulse by visiting a library. You get to take home something new and it doesn't cost anything!

Free entertainment. Family outings do not have to be expensive. Biking, hiking, visits to a park or playground, picnics, free concerts are just a few suggestions.

Move to an area with excellent public schools. Save the cost of private school tuition.

Trade toys. Find a family with kids about the same age as yours. Do a toy swap. "New" toys for free! (Save them up for Christmas and birthdays.) This works best with younger kids.

Take your own snacks to movies and ball games.

Go to a movie matinee. They're always cheaper!

Rent a movie instead of springing for tickets for the entire family.

Don't join record, CD or book clubs. You can do

much better at your local discount stores and you won't have to worry about sending back selections you didn't want.

When buying kids' clothes and shoes, set a budget figure and if the child wants to upgrade to a trendier brand or style, require her or him to pay the difference.

Perfect reverse psychology. Comes in handy as an effective way of steering adolescents away from expensive tastes.

Dream big. It's free!

Miscellaneous

Plant deciduous (lose their leaves in winter) trees on the south side of your house to provide summer shade without blocking winter sun. Plant evergreens on the north to shield your home from cold winter winds.

When staying in a hotel don't make phone calls from your room. Use the pay phone in the lobby and save at least 50 percent, even on your local calls.

Never buy new if used will do. Usually you pay less than half of new, won't have to pay sales tax on the new price, and will be kind to the environment.

Don't carry extra cash. Take along only as much money as you expect to need each day. Compulsive purchases are difficult to make with no dollars to spare.

Think positively. Think about how much you are

gaining from your cheapskate life-style, not what you are giving up.

Shop for a free checking account. Most banks have these if you ask. There may be certain stipulations, but usually they are quite easy to adhere to. Senior citizens are usually entitled to free accounts without limits.

When entertaining guests for a meal, spend time not money. The biggest compliment you can pay your dinner guests is to serve dishes that require more preparation than money. Anyone can grill an expensive steak or roast a rack of lamb, but few people make beef bourguignon, lasagna, soufflés, homemade breads, cheesecakes or other time-consuming dishes, despite how delicious and economical they can be. The hostess who goes to the trouble to prepare such delicacies gives her guests, her family and her spending plan a treat.

Vacation during off season. You can save big time on everything from travel to hotels and food.

Take up camping. Borrow or rent the gear.

Attend free concerts. Most cities have community sponsored entertainment during summer months. Many churches and colleges have free performances during holidays.

Work hard. Be a good employee, giving a full day's work for a full day's pay. Keep your job.

Be content with what you have. As much as possible, do not spend your life scheming and planning to get more things.

Never buy checks through your bank. You can save more than 50 percent by ordering direct.

Find a bank that doesn't charge a fee for ATM activity. If this is impossible, curb the urge to make many small transactions.

Take it back. If you bought something that you can't use, don't like or that is damaged—for heaven's sake, take it back. Retailers these days are quite anxious to make the customer happy by making adjustments, giving credit or cash refunds. Decide what you want and then stand up for yourself.

Have your pet neutered. Nursing, feeding and getting rid of litters is costly, both emotionally and financially.

Collect loose change. Make it a habit to dump your pockets and purses every night into one collection receptacle. You won't miss the change and you'll be amazed how much you can save.

Debt is a four letter word. As soon as you teach that to yourself, teach it to your children. Banish it from your life. (Debt here is understood to be unsecured consumer credit.)

Replace only if you cannot refurbish, repair, redo or get along without.

Clean your fine jewelry the same way you clean your fine teeth—with toothpaste, water and toothbrush.

Think bartering. Whenever possible trade goods or services instead of money; haircuts for typing, baby-sitting for landscape maintenance, or housecleaning for electrical work (just a few ideas).

Every purchase should pass a rigid scrutiny test. Do I really need it? Do I already have something that would make a suitable substitute? Am I certain I have located the very lowest price?

Do not carry credit cards. If you have to own them, keep them in a safe out-of-the-way place.

Any purchase that requires your signature probably requires payments. Think about it for 30-days before you sign. You just might have a change of heart. If not, then you probably will avoid buyer's remorse and feel confident in your decision.

The $100 Bill Trick

- We're funny creatures, we human beings! A long time ago I read that for some unexplainable reason, if a person keeps a $100 bill tucked away at home, he/she will be less likely to do lots of impulse buying.
  Now I don't know why this works, but I tried it, and believe me, just knowing the money is there (in a bill that is large enough to cause me not to want to break it) did something, and I found myself making fewer impulse purchases. I guess a psychologist would be able to explain the dynamics of this activity . . . it works for me!

CHAPTER 7

The Best of Cheapskate Monthly Selected Articles

THAT INFAMOUS THREAD

Following is a collection of quotes I have received from some of you over the past month. If you recognize yourself, go ahead and raise your hand. "No matter how much money I make, there is never enough." "We live from paycheck to paycheck, and constantly feel that we're just one pay period from being homeless." "I make $50,000 a year but I'm always broke." "I am so sick of living on the edge." "I know the embarrassment one feels when unpaid bills are creeping out of every crevice in the house." "Help! Help! I feel like I'm being eaten alive." "Every month I feel like I'm dangling from a tiny thread that's getting thinner and thinner. . . ." "The harder I work the 'behinder' I get. Will it ever get easier?"

You probably didn't notice, but I've been holding my hand up because I can identify with every single quote. I've been there and I've said those very things over and over.

Until the pain became unbearable, I was not willing to change. Pain brings change. Crisis precedes progress. And change exposes our weaknesses. No wonder so many of us avoid change at any cost!

I have a pretty clear inclination that the reason you have subscribed to *Cheapskate Monthly* is because finally the pain has become so great that you are now ready to make some changes.

It is not going to happen overnight—the change, I mean. But you can start right now.

First of all, acknowledge that it doesn't matter how much money you make. You don't believe me, I can tell. I know this is true because I get the same kinds of letters from people who make $12,000 a year and those who make $112,000. I was in far more financial pain when we were making good money than when we were first married and made "peanuts." It's not how much you make—it's how much you spend!

I've been thinking a lot about this and have come up with the following premise. Every expenditure falls into one of two categories: essential or optional.

Essential expenses are those items necessary for life. Brutal honesty pares down the typical essential list to:

Basic food
Basic clothing
Basic shelter

Basic transportation
Taxes
Insurance
Savings

I agree that by strict definition that list could be cut even further. But I prefer to think that an automobile and insurance required by law are essential. I also feel that saving is an essential expense. If your income does not cover these basic essentials (the operative word here is *basic)* you need to seriously consider how you can increase your income and in the meantime cut the essentials even more. I believe that for the majority of us, income does exceed the basic costs of preserving life.

The clever mind can find a way to manipulate an essential to include optional upgrades. For instance, basic shelter is essential. A million dollar estate overlooking the beach is optional. Basic clothing is essential, but that $2,000 Italian silk suit is optional. Weekly grocery shopping at Trader Joe's (or some other gourmet specialty store) can hardly be considered basic food.

And you thought only kids had to deal with peer pressure! Our homes, clothes and cars often reflect our dreams rather than the reality of our resources.

If the mortgage company approves a loan application we take this as a mandate from God that we can afford it. If the car dealer approves a new car loan, we breathe a sigh of relief—never questioning whether this new obligation is going to be manageable. Don't kid yourself—that salesperson is thinking of only one thing: commission.

We must start thinking for ourselves and taking control of our financial lives from the hands of people who couldn't care less whether the obligation can be met. And we really need to grow up and stop demanding to have things *now* that we really cannot afford.

An optional expense is an extra, an upgrade—something on your wish list. These are the things that enhance and enrich our lives. Optionals provide convenience and ease. Optionals are wonderful and I have many of them myself. But optionals must always be paid with optional funds—also known as *cash*. In our Premiere Issue I referred to this money as "spendable"—what is left over after all of your essentials have been paid.

Whenever you obligate yourself with money you don't have (another way to say "charge it"), you are turning an optional into an essential. An essential expense is something that must be paid every month without fail regardless of your current situation. This is the reason so many of us can't even pay our "bills" every month. Without much forethought we have managed to turn nonsensical items into essential expenses. When will this craziness end?

Here's an example: You need a new handbag. A handbag is a clothing item and is essential. You, however, feel that a Louis Vitton handbag is the purchase of choice. (Notice the manipulation and justification.) That particular upgrade should be considered an optional expense.

You don't have the exact cash to pay for the LV bag and so you put it on your department store credit card. In the same time it takes you to sign the credit slip, you have now made that bag an essential expense. You have to pay for it—you have no choice in the matter. And if you live in the perpetual state of perma-debt you will be paying for it for a long, long time. Far better to either buy a bag you can afford *or* wait until you can save enough cash for good old LV.

Every time you buy on credit you are converting optional purchases into essential expenses. Think about it. Every meal you pay for with plastic, every contract you sign at a health spa, a book club, a record club, a private school, a furniture store, a jewelry store, etc., is adding to your essential expenses list. And those items must be paid for every month come heck or high water! It is no longer a choice. You've put your neck on the line.

My personal goal is to become debt-free just as soon as possible. I want to cut our essential expenses down so low that regardless of the fickle economy, the current market or our current income we can live free from fear of financial disaster.

So why is your thread so thin? Maybe because your rope has been required to carry far too much weight for far too long. Make yourself a promise that you will start now to do everything you can to lighten the load.

PAY YOURSELF FIRST

I'm going to let you in on a secret which will revolutionize your life: *Save money.* Before you pay any of your bills, put something away. "Something" can be as little as $1.00, or ideally 10 percent of everything you make—that should be your goal. I recommend that you find a safe, secret place to begin your savings. It might be a cup on the top shelf or an envelope in a desk drawer. But start putting something away in your secret place. Do it every week. Without fail. As soon as you have $50.00 get it into a savings account. Keep depositing and *never withdraw.* Act as if you don't even have the money—no matter what. When you receive that $2.00 rebate back in the mail, put it into your account. Birthday money? Into the account. Before you know it, you will have a respectable balance. When it gets up around $1,000 (don't laugh—if you follow what I say, it will) start considering what is the wisest place for your investment. Remember, you can't start saving too soon, and no amount is too small!

ON BEING A TRUE CHEAPSKATE

I am certain that many of you have been completely turned off by the term *cheapskate* by now. At first, I was, too. But please hear me out. I had to come up with a term that implies the complete opposite of a spendthrift and I think "cheapskate" fits the bill. Give it time—it will grow on you.

There are several types of cheapskates. First there is the natural-born. This is a person who is just naturally thrifty, and probably never bounced a check, made a compulsive purchase or dove head-over-heels into debt. I am in awe of you natural-borns and please let the rest of us learn from you.

Next, there are the converted cheapskates. This is the category into which I fall. I was born into a naturally thrifty environment, not a wealthy family. I grew up observing and living a meager life-style. But it did not "stick." I must have been a natural-born spendthrift. But I am a living example that conversion is possible.

Cheapskates come in all varieties, too. I do not personally advocate a "bag lady" style. I don't collect cans along the beach, or go through industrial trash bins. But you should see me stretch a dollar at the grocery store. I don't cram my philosophy down anyone's throat, and I don't impose my personal style on family or friends. I like to think that I am a classy, dignified cheapskate. For example, I would prefer one very nice outfit rather than ten from the thrift store. I would rather live frugally 50 weeks of the year to allow for a nice family vacation. I am more interested in finding new ways to save cash, cut medical/auto insurance costs, open my own money market account with $100, learn how to keep my car in good repair for the very least amount of money than in (for example) saving egg cartons, hoping to think of some meaningful use! The thought of buying a piece of income-producing property is far more exciting to me (and I will!) than recycling aluminum foil. But that's just me.

I am so proud to be a cheapskate and excited to share this way of life with you and others of like mind.

HOW'S YOUR ATTITUDE

I know myself well enough to admit that my attitude is directly related to my bank account balance. The smaller the balance, the worse the attitude and likewise the higher the balance the easier it is to face each day with a positive attitude.

The easiest way to maintain a winning attitude is to have cash in an account. Sounds pretty simple— and pretty impossible at the same time. But it is not impossible. The less money you have, the more important it is that you pay yourself first! Make it a personal challenge to pay yourself 10 percent of every paycheck first. Just do it. If you wait until you have 10 percent extra, you will never start. Make this your attitude account. Do this even when you do not have enough left over to pay everyone else. Believe me, they will still be around next month. In your effort to repay your debtors it is essential that you have a good attitude.

Even during the very worst financially stressful months, your 10 percent attitude money—your mental shelter—is going to get you through. Never, never touch your attitude account. Make a commitment to yourself in writing that you will not touch the money for overdue bills, emergencies or any other logical reason! You will find that your attitude will stabilize and will get you past your short-term financial dilemmas.

ANATOMY OF A SUPERMARKET

I never thought much about the logistics and intense marketing genius behind a supermarket business and all of the subliminal aspects until one day, in a tremendous hurry, I dashed into my favorite market only to find they had completely rearranged the entire place the previous night. How dare they mess with my mind. The harder I searched for the items I needed, the more frustrated I became. In my usual timid manner, I went directly to the store manager to register my complaint and was told that this is just business as usual for a profit conscious modern day supermarket. In frustration I stormed out with only part of what I had intended to purchase.

Later on, when I had regained my composure, I went back and had a very enlightening conversation with the manager. It seems that a store of this magnitude has a pretty high overhead and allocates a large portion of its advertising budget to finding ways to appeal to the customer's compulsive shopping habits.

It has been proven that the typical shopper soon memorizes the layout of the store, knows exactly where to find the items needed and in a short time becomes oblivious to products not regularly purchased. But turning the place upside down every year or so, the store can "introduce" its regular shoppers to thousands of products they might never have noticed had the order of the store not been disturbed. And to be ever so much more helpful, the merchandising experts determined that larger shopping carts would be nice. Ever notice how much larger those carts are than they were ten years ago? They know that we shop till the cart's full! I can only imagine what they are planning for the future. Maybe motorized carts complete with rearview mirror, turn signals and optional trailer—all for the shopper's convenience, of course.

The average food shopper spends over an hour every week in a semicomatose state shuffling up and down the aisles of the all-American supermarket snatching item after item, building an expensive tower in a basket. At the end of the exercise the score is tallied and in most cases the supermarket is the clear winner. The ordinary shopper is as predictable as a rat following a trail of cheese right into a trap.

The most expensive and frivolous items are usually placed at eye level. Baking staples like flour and sugar are usually on low shelves or so high up you have trouble reaching them.

Eye-catching displays with lights, bells and whistles usually are promoting junk-type and very expensive items even though they are piled up to appear to be on sale.

The center aisles usually house the prepared and overprocessed brightly packaged food items. The perimeter of the store is the safe zone—produce, dairy and meat. Either a hot-deli or bakery in the store will be emitting heavenly smells to appeal to your senses and start those compulsive buying juices flowing.

Remember—you can't avoid the supermarket completely and it is very difficult to remain completely true to your shopping list and financial plan in these kinds of stores. But you can commit to doing regular shopping in a no-frills warehouse store and enter the supermarket with extreme *caution*, fully aware of the many ways your compulsiveness is being tested.

It's a pretty safe bet that food shopping will be more than an optional pastime for the rest of your life. You have two choices: either lapse into an even deeper comatose state or get smart!

SUFFERING EMPLOYMENT INSECURITY?

It seems that the words *job* and *security* really do not go together anymore. All you need to do is pick up today's paper—any paper, and read which company has just completed another major layoff. Here is today's headline in my paper: "GM loses $4.5 billion, cuts to the bone; firm to close plants, slash 74,000 jobs; workers in shock."

I don't know about you, but I would much prefer a root canal without benefit of anesthesia to a blind side unemployment hit!

These days unemployment has absolutely no respect. It is hunting down elite executives just the same as clerical and factory workers. Unemployment does not seem to be singling out any one particular part of the country, either. Forecasters of employment trends don't seem to be predicting any imminent change in the situation.

So what's the answer? Give in to the Big Three *W*s? . . . uh, that's wish, whine and worry . . . or hold a pity party? Probably not, even though that attitude feels surprisingly comfortable once in a while.

Try this analogy: I live in California where the threat of earthquakes is pretty high. But I still live here voluntarily, and so do a lot of others! Certain areas of the East Coast live with the seasonal threat of hurricanes. But I don't see those areas becoming unpopulated any time soon. We have learned to prepare for these disasters. My kids learned "duck and cover" right along with fire drills from the first day of preschool. We have certain disaster plans in place —just in case. New California laws require every employer to have a safety manual in the event someone just happens to accidentally drink copier toner! My point is that we prepare for the most remote of potential disasters while leaving ourselves completely open to more likely crises!

Wise persons should prepare for unemployment. In fact everyone should—there are no guarantees for tomorrow. Rather than reacting to devastation with shock, I think a proactive posture seems far more appropriate.

Workplace Trends, an Ohio newsletter for management types, says that job security for both blue-collar and white-collar workers was a phenomenon which occurred after World War II and is now history. Today's corporate executive can plan to change employers on the average of seven times during his or her career—and not all voluntarily.

So I would like to unveil the Official Cheapskate Employment Disaster Preparedness Plan. Nothing new—just some focused common sense.

I. Do Everything Necessary to Stay Employed:

1. Consider your job a blessing. Obviously this is easier for some than others! If you "think thankfulness" for your employer you might actually start feeling that way.

2. Step up your savings program. Experts say

you need the equivalent of three to six months' expenses set aside for possible loss of employment. In your dreams? You can do it! At the very minimum you should have six weeks' expenses set aside—it will take that long to start receiving unemployment benefits.

3. Become an expert on which alternative employment possibilities are available. Read the jobs available sections of the classifieds religiously to keep educated.

4. Start a file on employment alternatives. Learn what additional requirements you might need should you make a future career change.

5. Update your resume—just in case. It's not a bad idea to review and update it every six months.

6. At the first sign of serious weakness in your industry or firm, step up your job search. Whatever you do, don't quit one job until you have landed another.

7. Make your decision to change jobs as unemotionally as possible. Trade in your nerves for excitement—two closely related emotions.

8. Weigh your decisions carefully. Don't not make a change just because you feel obligated to go down with a sinking ship.

II. In the Event of Unemployment:

1. Don't panic. Those who love and depend on you need you to stay calm and smart.

2. Don't pay off your debts with severance pay, stock plans or any lump sums you might have received upon separation from your employer. You're going to need these sources for living essentials.

3. Determine how long you can hold out using your cash to cover the bare necessities. This will give you a clear picture of what you need to do.

4. Call your creditors immediately. I mean everyone—even your landlord or mortgage holder. Be very honest and up-front about your situation.

5. Make a job hunting plan. Network! You just never know when Aunt Susie's hairdresser's husband's boss's sister-in-law's nephew might be looking for someone with your exact qualifications.

6. Keep a positive attitude—even if you have to fake it for a while.

7. Consider taking temporary employment provided it is in your field or profession.

8. Remember: Everything is going to be OK!

UNBEND YOUR BOW

Ever feel like a hamster on an exercise wheel that is never going to stop? The faster you run, the faster the wheel goes and so you have to run faster and then that makes the wheel go faster and . . . I don't think I am alone in admitting that my life-style gives an open invitation to major *stress*.

In my top desk drawer I keep a little booklet. It is exactly 23 pages long and the size of a wallet. It is titled simply *Stress*.* Let me quote the first paragraph:

"There is an old Greek motto that says: 'You will break the bow if you keep it always bent.' Wise words, but how do we loosen the strings? Even when we make every effort to slow down and relax, others place high demands on us. Their 'shoulds' and 'oughts' and 'musts' hit us like strong gusts of wind, driving our lives onto shallow reefs of frustrations and even desperation.''

Broken bows come in all forms. Hospital emergency rooms, broken relationships, bouncing from one job to another—the list goes on and on. But there is an alternative. There are ways to unbend the bow regularly so that when it is tightened it has the give and spring necessary to do its job.

It is when my life gets out of balance that the stress mounts to unmanageable heights. It has not been a quick or easy task to get into balance. And I'm not there yet—but I have made good progress. I no longer work twelve-hour days. I am learning to trust others to assist me. I have taken up hobbies

* *Stress: Calm Answers for the Worry Worn.* Charles R. Swindoll. Copyright 1981 Charles R. Swindoll, Inc. (Multnomah Press, Portland, OR 97266)

again. I am actually excited about cross-stitch and quilting! I have learned that there is always time to do those things that are really important. It is just a matter of making those choices of priority.

So why don't you try it just for today—go ahead and unbend your bow. Slow down. Smile at the future. Resign from some of your obligations that are weighing you down, those things that are robbing you of peace and joy. Take up a hobby. Do one thing this weekend that is completely out of your character. You'll be surprised how powerful your bow will be on Monday morning when you string it back up!

THE CHEAPSKATE PHILOSOPHY

Needless to say, this whole newsletter thing is bringing much attention, many comments and questions —mostly related to this zany word *cheapskate.*

There really isn't a good word in our language for a reformed spendthrift. So I had two choices: either create a brand-new word (couldn't think of one) or redefine something already in the dictionary. (I redefined.) Sorry, Mr. Webster, but I like mine better.

Cheapskates do not spend more money than they actually have. One of those things we were supposed to learn in kindergarten, I believe. They live within their means. Isn't it peculiar how our life-style or standard of living seems to always be just a little bit higher than our income? Things can be going along touch-and-go, paycheck-to-paycheck style. Then, just in the nick of time, you get a very much needed and equally deserved raise or discover an income tax refund is due and breathe a sigh of relief. But before you ever see the additional income, something happens to eat that up too, and so you find yourself right back in the just-a-little-bit-short spot once again. There is a better way!

A cheapskate:

1. Above all else, saves 10 percent of all income.

2. Does not buy compulsively, but makes intelligent and well-thought-out choices.

3. Earns more money than he spends no matter how desperate or tempting the situation might appear.

4. Has a spirit of generosity, giving away time, talent and assets.

5. Lives within a financial plan which includes margin to allow for spontaneity and fun.

6. Can easily become ecstatic over a real bargain or frugal find.

7. Lives honestly and ethically no matter the temptation to do otherwise in order to get a better deal.

That's it! Nothing negative or shameful. Being a cheapskate is honorable. You see—there is absolutely nothing wrong with having nice things, or having dreams and goals for achievement and success. It is when we demand the right to have things *now* by diving head-over-heels into debt through the improper use of credit, that we get into big trouble.

This is a philosophy—a model or standard. I can't imagine there is a perfect cheapskate anywhere. If there is, I need to hear from you.

Writing about this every day, reading your letters and talking to a lot of people (you have to remember that up until four months ago, "My Story" was pretty much a big secret unknown to anyone but my husband!) has just propelled me miles down the recovery road. Sure, we've been through some very tough years. I still can't believe how far we've come —and the last thing I ever thought I would do is actually admit it to anyone.

But taking the plunge and telling all has had a remarkably positive effect on me. It is a humbling thought that one should only preach what one practices.

Having a compulsive personality, I tend to dive headfirst into everything I do. And this newsletter has been no exception. Spending many hours reading and writing on this subject has demanded that I become even more focused and committed to achieving our financial goals, becoming debt-free and having greater economic freedom. My readers are looking over my shoulder!

RECESSION RECOVERY

Whether you are experiencing a simple economic downturn, or a full-blown recession, everyone is feeling the pinch. I think we all agree that this will eventually end—recessions always do. But how soon? How quickly? Who really knows? Everything I read leads me to believe that recovery will be slow and halting.

The danger, however, is that many American families will go on doing business as usual, not having learned from past experiences. Many will return to the habits of the 1980s—spend! spend! spend!

Plan now and anticipate the probably short-lived economic recovery as a time to continue to pay off debt, build up reserves and keep finding new ways to cut spending. Prepare for what many wise economists are predicting will be a much more severe recession to follow this one.

Don't become discouraged. On the contrary, be encouraged that you have shown the wisdom and fortitude to do something about your financial situation now. We will have an opportunity and probably soon, to take advantage of a good economic time. That should be plenty of time, if used wisely, to make the necessary plans and preparations for personal financial survival!

GETTING ORGANIZED

Putting your household in order might just result in cash in your pocket and a new smile on your face. . . . Have you ever:

- Not answered the phone because you couldn't find it?
- Thrown away an entire Tupperware container because the contents had been in the back of the fridge so long that replacing seemed preferable to cleaning?
- While searching for the Valentine centerpiece, stumbled over the Christmas wrap purchased at the 50 Percent Off After Holiday Sale two years ago?
- Discovered that you have a warehouse full of partially full peanut butter jars in the pantry?
- Found the 12-month-size baby shower gifts in the closet, only to realize baby Huey is already busting out of the 24-month size?
- Written a phone message on the wall? With an eyebrow pencil?
- Held to the philosophy that a gritty bathtub is much safer than a sparkling clean, slippery one?
- Ended up giving a brand-new shirt to Goodwill because you lost the sales receipt and just never got around to taking it back for exchange?
- Gone out to dinner for the sole reason that there wasn't one clean dish in the house?

Getting organized is like dieting. Everyone knows how, has several favorite methods, and is pretty crazy about the results. The problem is just getting around to doing it.

Remember that wonderful feeling of accomplishment the last time you thoroughly and honestly cleaned and reorganized a closet? We recently redecorated our kitchen and went so far as to completely empty every cupboard and drawer. When everything was finished and it was time to put everything back, I decided to put things away only as I used them. I quickly realized why it was such a problem to keep the kitchen neat and tidy; we just had too much stuff, most of which had not been used in years. Getting rid of the unused stuff left so much more space in which to organize the essentials.

Face it. If you don't have enough closet, drawer and storage space to comfortably handle your possessions, you probably own too many things. Give away, pare down, and let your rooms, closets and drawers appear serenely controlled—kept! Eliminate! Concentrate! Be disciplined!

Getting organized is surely not the end-all. And there is no "right" way to do things, unless it's right for you. Organization must fit your style, your energy and your schedule. Find a system that functions best for you and your family. Beware of extremes where the appointment book, budget and expenditure records, filing systems, and master lists take more time than just working out the problems they were intended to solve. (Exception: Your lifetime spending record!)

Where to start? Getting rid of clutter is a good place. There's an old adage: "A place for everything and everything in its place." No doubt about it— getting rid of things you own involves risk. But here's a promise: You won't ever get rid of something that's absolutely essential to your life. As you assess each overstuffed area, consider selling your excess or donating to a charity in exchange for a tax receipt.

People who have problems with clutter are very careful individuals, indeed. Personally, however, I feel that these individuals are quite wonderful—we are a cut above the average! We're creative, intelligent, nice people. We just need to learn to let go— live a little, take the plunge.

You might like to try what I call the Grocery Bag Method for instant results, taught to me by a very clever friend, Jan Sandberg. This works best at about 8:00 P.M. when you are at your wit's end over the endless clutter and chaotic appearance of your home. Take one (more as necessary) large brown paper grocery bag and fill it with all of the stacks of extraneous papers, magazines, mail—your basic clutter. The purpose here is not to throw anything away, but just to get it out of visual range until you have time to go through and separate, sort and file. (This is what you tell yourself!)

Now, if within 48 hours or so (give or take a month) no one in the family has mentioned missing something of importance, it is probably safe to go ahead and throw the whole thing out. This is not a highly recommended method, but it does work!

A much preferred way to get organized is the Salami Method. You wouldn't think of eating an entire salami at one sitting would you? You would eat it in slices over some period of time. Just start with one thing, one room, one closet. Tomorrow is another day, another drawer, another attic. Soon you'll be in control, one space at a time.

As we gain control of our things, we're going to feel more in control of our lives and that will be reflected in our attitudes. Just think of all the ways your life is affected by your attitude!

I've been doing a lot of reading and researching on this whole topic of organization. This includes housekeeping, office keeping, time management— your basic living in order rather than in chaos. There are terrific resources at your local library or bookstore. I'm pretty much convinced there is a method and idea for every personality type living under any circumstance.

You'll be happy to hear that the ratio of natural-born neatniks to brilliant, exciting, wonderful messies is about one in a million. We are definitely in the majority!

It's spring and the earth is renewing itself with fresh, clean life. There couldn't be a better time to start than now. Take a risk—clean out your purse or briefcase. If you have a call to make, start dialing. A closet to dig out? Get to shoveling. A salami to tackle? Start slicing.

P.S. One of my staff has politely pointed out to me how ironic it is to see me preparing this issue on organization while seated in the midst of a very disorderly and basically messy-beyond-belief office. Why doesn't anyone believe that this is my very own unique filing system? I'm so convicted that as soon as this issue is out, I'm getting this place organized!

CHEAPSKATE TO GO UNDERCOVER

It happened again last night. It happens a lot. The phone rang about 9:15 P.M. A very excited, vivacious young voice on the other end asked excitedly, "Is this Mary Hunt . . . Mary M. Hunt?" An affirmative yet suspicious answer encouraged him to continue.

"You're not going to believe this but you are definitely the winner of one of six fabulous prizes and the least valuable is a twenty-inch color TV!"

I really didn't want him to go on. I very rudely asked what this was all about and what did I have to do to claim my prize. You probably know the rest. All that is required is to attend a very low-key sales presentation at a lovely local hotel and voila! a new TV—"at the very least."

I did as I have done at least a hundred times before. I told him I wasn't interested. My curt response was the result of hearing about these gimmicks from friends and relatives coupled with years of experience in blowing out these annoying evening calls. Just who are these guys anyway?

I have made a decision, however, that the next time I get "the call" I am going to go for it because I now feel a responsibility to find out once and for all just what these people are after. My logical mind says that there is no free lunch and so no one is going to just give me a free TV. Some way someone wants me to buy something. And they want it very badly. I am going to find out just what happens from the first call on.

So the next time I am notified that I am a winner, I am going to act thoroughly surprised and thrilled. I am going to attend whatever meeting is required and all the time I am going to take copious notes. The reason I will be going undercover to one of these functions is to find out the *truth* and then report back to you, my dear readers. Hopefully, my experiences will either lay to rest once and for all my suspicions or expose misleading sales tactics. I've always thought that if it is too good to be true, it probably is!

So be patient. It might take a while for them to get around to me again. But when they do, they'd better beware because I intend to find out everything possible about this whole method of telemarketing—not for me (of course), but for you, my readers. I promise that I will not spend a penny and will not enter into any kind of contract—verbal or written. And what will I do with the prize? Maybe we can barter!

Last minute update: I got another call on Memorial Day! This organization is just a little too anxious for comfort. Oh, well—as promised I excitedly agreed and have my big appointment on June 6. Report forthcoming . . .

MISSION ACCOMPLISHED!

The day was Saturday, June 6, 1992. It was a beautiful, warm California morning and getting up to keep an appointment was not quite my first choice of activities. However, I had made a commitment and besides, who wouldn't make the effort to get a new 20 inch color TV, "at the very least"?

Heather, the salesperson who originally called, together with subsequent follow-up mail pieces (they could hardly be called letters because they had that distinctive junk-mail look) reiterated that all married attendees must be accompanied by their spouse. So Harold reluctantly agreed to go along. Anything for a new TV.

We left in plenty of time to ensure a prompt arrival. Detailed instructions led us to a very posh new office building on Fashion Island right across from Neiman-Marcus in "bucks up" Newport Beach, California. As we approached in our white Nissan we immediately noticed the Mercedes-Benzes, BMWs and Jaguars strategically parked at the entrance.

Valet attendants dashed up to both doors treating us somewhat like royalty.

As we opened the large double glass doors, directly in front of us was a huge beautiful counter with several very attractive dressed-for-success, bubbly ladies attending. I stopped momentarily to make mental notes of the decor. Everything was shiny and new, done in brass and mauve tones with a lot of mirrors. The furniture was all very well coordinated and strategically placed to allow for clusters of three persons to engage in intimate conversation. Upbeat yet inoffensive music was playing at just the perfect volume. It was clear that nothing was left out in putting together a very enticing and inviting atmosphere.

We were seated and told that our representative would be with us shortly. As we sat down we noticed the very large lighted photo boxes on the walls. These huge pictures showed gorgeous people vacationing all over the world. All were dressed perfectly, had perfect bodies and perfect hair blowing in the perfect wind. Obviously, they had no cares in the world.

Our stay at this location was just long enough to make us picture ourselves in those scenes. I knew it was time to take out my small notebook.

Just at that moment up walked our wonderful new friend, Tony. Tony was dressed to the nines in a beautiful suit, Italian shoes, understated gold bracelet and watch and a smile that could melt steel. His jacket was casually slung over his shoulder and hung just so on a hook which doubled as his right index finger. Tony inquired about our morning so far and then invited us into the theater (properly pronounced the'-a-tuh).

This large room was equally gorgeous with luxurious theater seats all done in mauve velvet, plush carpet and ultramodern electronic video equipment built into the walls. A huge screen was straight ahead and quickly all of the reps made sure that their couple was comfortably seated. I hadn't seen that many smiles or felt that kind of excited energy in quite a while.

The lights dimmed and the movie began. Beautiful music preceded some great photography of famous parts of the world. And then enter: Robin Leach! He and his gorgeous nameless female companion had just one message: "Yes, you too can be part of the world of the rich and famous!"

Everything was so well-done, so slick, so believable. I didn't get caught up in it though because I was madly taking notes in the dark—trying to get down everything going on around me. In about twenty minutes the movie faded out, the lights faded back—all in sync with the large sets of double brass doors which gracefully opened automatically and without a sound.

We were immediately rejoined by Tony and taken into a large room set up as a patio/garden. There were dozens of small white round patio tables with three chairs each. I immediately noticed the smell of fresh, hot buttered popcorn (a bit unusual for a Saturday morning). Each table was decorated with three balloons and there were potted trees and plants throughout—quite a lovely and relaxing atmosphere.

We sat down and Tony asked how we liked the movie and if we could enjoy that kind of life.

Who could say no? He served us fresh lemonade and popcorn and just happened to mention that he had "just returned from the south of France," "Had met his lovely Dutch wife while vacationing in Spain the year before" and proceeded to whip out the wedding album to prove it!

Ahhhhhhh—it might have sounded quite inviting if I had not been so preoccupied with my notebook. Tony did ask why I was taking notes. I told him I wanted to be able to remember all the details.

About this time Tony practiced some "reverse snobbery" for the first time. It was flawlessly executed and went like this: "If you feel that these kinds of vacations don't fit into your life-style, we can end right now and you can get your prize and be on your way." No one—not even a cheapskate, takes well to that kind of thing. We declined because I had more facts to learn. I had a mission to complete.

We finally learned that this company (and there are many, many such companies out there) markets condominium projects with a slight twist. On this day they were selling two projects—one in Dana Point and one in San Diego, both California.

Each condo—there are 102 in the Dana Point

project—will be sold fifty-one times . . . did you hear me? Fifty-one times! . . . and each owner will have a deed and title to $1/51$ of the condo and the right to occupy it one week each year. I did a little mental calculation and figured they would be trying to sell us 15 square foot of condo. My closet is bigger than that.

We were quickly educated that the privilege of ownership includes three additional weeks per year to be spent at any of the hundreds of similar resort locations throughout the world at a mere $99–$349 per week. Sounds great, doesn't it? Who could resist? (I'll tell you who: Anyone smart enough to realize those numbers don't allow any transportation to get to the Fiji Islands.)

By this time we were getting into the details of the sale and so I pulled out my trusty calculator. Tony was pretty concerned about this. These kinds of sales tactics are terribly threatened by facts and figures. I guess that's why they wish to avoid too many details.

By the time we had completed the two hours, Tony had tried the reverse snobbery thing three more times, and had called his broker over two different times to close us. Broker Cy, bedecked with massive gold and jewels was a much slicker package than Tony. I was pretty sure we had received all the information they were going to part with.

The whole sales pitch attempted to be very low-key and laid-back but was in fact extremely high-pressured in a subtle way. Passive-aggressive is an apt description, I believe. However, at the very end, as we were being pressured to sign "today" in order to get all of the bonuses, I told Tony that I would never buy something sight unseen. I asked if there were tours available at the Dana Point project. His response was that this was not at all necessary, since the point of ownership is to travel all over the world enjoying everything "for free" (which he said more than a few times), not to vacation forever in Dana Point!

When Tony and Cy finally heard the word no on our twelfth try, we were quickly shown to a less glitzy hallway which led to a plain white counter area where the employees without personality handed us our prize. Our fondest dreams would have been fulfilled with the very least valuable of all the prizes available—a 20 inch color TV. But no . . . we had to win one of the most valuable prizes—four nights and three days in Las Vegas! The certificates give no hotel name or transportation details *and* require a $50.00 deposit to participate. In small print it says "subject to availability" and you know what that means.

I understand that this kind of sales activity is going on all over the country, usually by mail but sometimes by phone. I hesitate to make a blanket judgment. However my common sense tells me that if these are such wonderful investments, why do they have to trick us into a pressure packed sales presentation?

On the whole, I recommend you avoid this type of

thing at all costs. Your time is too valuable. If you are blessed with resources to allow for lavish travel you sure don't need these clowns to make the arrangements.

Here are the screaming red flags we noticed. Should you find yourself in a similar situation you might want to keep this as a list of deadly symptoms to steer clear of to avoid making a terrible mistake.

1. Overboard attempt to impress with wealth and the good life. The valet parking, the fancy cars, gold and diamonds, slick photography and celebrities.

2. Subtle hooks which appeal to fantasies and compulsions. The good life, getting something for nothing, you deserve nice vacations, do it now while you can still enjoy it, you owe it to your kids!

3. Enjoy now and pay later. Only 10 percent down, deferred escrow fees, this low monthly payment will be mere pennies to you in a few years, etc.

4. Unreasonable and unrealistic statistics. Fifty-one owners paying huge sums each to own nothing more than a hotel suite, hundreds of resorts all over the world at your beck and call—subject to availability of course.

5. Undisclosed information. Homeowners' dues do not include property taxes, project is not exactly on the waterfront, must use their

financing, total number of units, exact locations, etc.

6. Must sign *today*. Don't ever let anyone tell you that you can't go home and think about it! They know that 99 percent of the time you won't come back.

I can't imagine a worse investment than the one we were presented. Remember, though, that it was masked by glowing terms and subtle nuances. It could be very tempting to the unsuspecting. *Beware!*

Epilogue. Five days after attending I did some more research. After making seven phone calls to seven different numbers I finally found that the Dana Point project is actually located in Capistrano Beach; tours are not conducted; if you take the exciting Las Vegas trip you stay at either the King-8 Hotel or Townhall Casino. Has anyone ever even heard of these places? Midweek only—subject to availability, and the $50.00 must be paid within 30 days. The first subscriber to request can have my complete exciting Las Vegas vacation if you promise to give us a detailed report . . . and good luck!

Note: My exhaustive research on this matter revealed that a typical two-bedroom condo with a view in Dana Point currently ranges from $150,000 to $400,000 and that is being very generous! These clowns are selling one condo for $1,085,790.00! Give me a break. I figured that this great buy would cost us

$5,519.86 per year for the first seven years. Sure that includes a couple of weeks' vacation lodging but no transportation, food or spending money. Tell me what kind of a bargain that is!

WANT TO SAVE MORE? $PEND LESS!

I won't bore you with the statistics, but it is staggering how many young American families have no method of saving money. On the contrary, it has become our way of life to spend every penny we make, living month after month depressed and bewildered about where all the money goes.

We race through our days at breakneck speed and our busy lives then become our justification for spending even more on goods and services necessary to further promote our hectic life-styles! Whew! Haven't you had just about enough?

Was the brand-new car really worth it? The five rooms of furniture you got such a great deal on— and with only 60 E-Z payments—is it starting to look a little tired and out of sorts? Too bad you still have two years to go on those payments. Remember the school clothes you bought with your nifty credit card last September? Any chance they'll be paid off by the time school starts in the fall?

Here's the truth in a nutshell: Every dollar you spend is a dollar you can't save. It's that simple! If you remember nothing else from this article, please remember that.

Last January I challenged you to start saving—paying yourself first! After all, who deserves it more? One reader said the only thing she could save was the change she found under the sofa cushions and in the laundry! Hey, that's a start. I want to get you thinking about saving rather than spending.

Now let's get beyond the nickels and dimes. You need to be putting away dollars, consistently, every month. I want savings to become a very high priority in your life. I can just hear you now: "But how can I save when I don't even have enough to pay my bills?" You just *do it*. You pay your savings first. In the beginning it may be a small amount. But that $5.00 is going to be $10.00 next month, and on and on.

I just have to throw some statistics in here. Did you know that 95 out of 100 Americans will retire on nothing more than Social Security? Seniors today living on those checks alone are forced to exist somewhere close to the poverty level. That means that 95 percent of the population must not be saving.

There are only four ways I know of to spend less and thereby free up more dollars to be saved:

Make things last longer
Use smaller quantities
Buy cheaper
Use a cheaper substitute

Sounds pretty simplistic—and it really is. What is difficult is dealing with our ingrained habits and attitudes regarding just what is necessary.

So, before you spend (which does include buying on credit) stop, think, and then think some more. Is there another way you can accomplish what it is you need? Can you make what you have last just a little longer? Can you find it cheaper somewhere else? Can you find a suitable alternative?

If after you go through this kind of analysis you do end up buying, make sure it is the best deal possible and then enjoy your purchase.

CLEANING ON THE CHEAP

The way I see it you have two options. Clean yourself or hire someone to do it for you. If you are one to hire out your housekeeping chores, you're on your own; I have no advice other than good luck. If on the other hand you are a do-it-yourselfer, I can help you save a bundle!

A word about cleaning. I approach it as a necessary evil; something I hate to do, but am driven to diligence by the results. Can you think of anything as lovely as a clean house with twinkling windows? Add fresh dried-in-the-outdoors bed sheets and I'm in heaven!

I was not always so gung ho on this subject. Years ago I got caught up with the glamour of hiring domestic help and with reckless abandon shelled out a lot of money only to end up with less than satisfactory results. When we started slashing our expenses, of course this luxury was the first to go and I took back the housekeeping responsibilities. Now I proudly align myself with those who cherish a good pumice stone and exalt the virtues of a genuine feather duster. But expensive glitzy cleaning supplies? No way! Why would I part with large sums of money to buy ready-made, when I can easily make superior products right in my own kitchen—for a fraction of the cost? It is not hard and takes very little time. Read on—I think you will agree!

A Few Words Before Getting Started

You must heed this one CAUTION. NEVER MIX CHLORINE BLEACH WITH ANYTHING OTHER THAN WATER. Chlorine bleach mixed with ammonia or any number of other items can result in toxic fumes which could have serious, if not fatal, results.

If the country pine or windsurf fragrances of some overpriced cleaning supplies are important to you—add potpourri or fancy room freshener to your shopping list. For the most part these products do not smell so wonderful. But their odoriferous qualities are short-lived and tell me—what smells better than "clean?"

The four basic items you will need to keep your home sparkling clean are: white vinegar, baking soda, ammonia (sudsing and nonsudsing), and isopropyl (rubbing) alcohol. These are ordinary products found in any market and they can be purchased cheaply.

White Vinegar: Dissolves hard water minerals and lime; cuts through soapy films, a nonabrasive cleanser.

Ammonia: Strong grease cutter; removes wax and finishes. Smells terrible.

Baking Soda: A mild, nonabrasive cleanser; neutralizes odors and acts as a booster for detergents.

Rubbing Alcohol: Acts as a solvent and dissolves sticky substances; disinfects and dissolves grime.

Here are my favorite cleaning supply recipes. You will see that there are several window cleaning formulas, for instance. But not all window dirt is created equal. Sometimes you will be dealing with hard water deposits, other times with grimy, greasy dirt! So the need will dictate the formula.

All-Purpose Window Cleaner

Into a plastic gallon jug mix:

$1/2$ C ammonia

$1/3$ C vinegar

2 tbl baking soda

Water (enough to fill jug)

Label, cap tightly and keep out of reach of children. Use in handy-dandy spray bottle.

Window Cleaner (when you have hard water marks and minerals)

Fill spray bottle with white vinegar—straight. Works even better if vinegar is heated.

All-Purpose Cleaner
   $1/2$ rubbing alcohol
   $1/2$ ammonia

That's all. Make up any amount you desire. Label and keep capped tightly and out of reach of children.

Little Known Uses for Everyday Household Products

Talk about cheap substitutes! You may well be able to get rid of all your fancy packaged, expensive household cleaners, trinkets and gadgets when you learn how to use every day ordinary old-fashioned basic down-to-earth commodities—available at your local market for very little money! And if you are concerned about removing toxic and environmentally hazardous things from your home, you're in for a double treat!

Ordinary Table Salt

Boil eggs in salty water and they'll peel easily.

Drop peeled apples, pears and potatoes in cold, lightly salted water and they won't turn brown.

To clean a really greasy pan first put salt in it and wipe it with a paper towel.

Cleaning tarnished silver will be easy if you rub the tarnish with salt before washing.

Rub your fingers with salty water to take away onion smell.

Salt can deodorize thermoses and other closed containers. It also works with smelly sneakers or any other canvas shoe.

Cream will whip better and egg whites will beat faster if you add a pinch of salt.

A pinch of salt added to the dry coffee grounds will take away the bitterness of a fresh cup of brewed coffee!

Add a pinch of salt to a carton of milk to keep it fresh longer.

New brooms will wear longer if soaked in hot salted water before first use.

Rub a thin paste of salad oil and salt on those white rings on your wood furniture. Let it stand an hour or two, then wipe it off. No more rings.

To remove perspiration stains, add four tablespoons of salt to one quart of hot water and sponge the fabric with solution until stains disappear.

If your iron leaves sticky black spots on your clothes, run the hot iron over a piece of paper on which is sprinkled a little salt. The crud will fall right off.

To whiten your teeth, remove plaque and promote healthy gums, mix one part salt and two parts baking soda after pulverizing the salt in a blender or rolling it on a cutting board with a heavy glass or mug. Sprinkle on your toothbrush and go to it.

If your goldfish are lethargic and grumpy put them in a quart of fresh water with a teaspoon of salt and let them swim around for fifteen minutes. Be sure and transfer them back to fresh water. They'll be perky and happy.

Rubbing Alcohol

Rubbing alcohol, because it kills malodorous bacteria, will eliminate offensive body odor from armpits and feet and any other odor producing bodily area!

Sticky labels on glass, mirrors or plastic containers come off easily with rubbing alcohol.

Removes hard-water stains on faucets; grease and fingerprints from chrome, enamel and stainless steel.

Keep a spray bottle of rubbing alcohol in kitchen for disinfecting knives, the cutting board after working with poultry or meat, the telephone, doorknobs and any little cuts you may get while chopping or slicing food.

Clean even the finest pearls with rubbing alcohol.

Makes a great fly/insect spray! (Fine mist evaporates quickly and is not harmful to anyone but the pest.) Be sure to wipe them up and dispose of before they wake up. Often this is only a potent anesthetic!

Great on grass and dye stains instead of expensive spot remover.

Shines chrome like crazy!

Fill a pump spray bottle and use it to control mealybugs on houseplants.

Removes hair spray buildup on curling irons.

Clean candles by wiping them with rubbing alcohol.

Clean paint brushes of shellac and shellac-based products.

Mix 3-1 with water for a floor wax remover.

Clean silicone caulking around bathtubs.

Dampen a rag and clean sanded surfaces prior to applying stain or finish.

Use to clean freezer shelves. Won't freeze as water-based product would.

Baking Soda

Baking soda is a nonabrasive cleanser. Use it without worry on fine china, porcelain appliances, the inside of your refrigerator, stainless steel, aluminum and cast iron.

Sprinkle baking soda all over a stuffed animal that cannot be laundered. Leave this "shower" on a few minutes, shake, dust off and fluff up with an old brush.

Remove crayon marks from walls by scrubbing gently with a paste of baking soda and water. An old toothbrush works great as a scrubber.

Line kitty litter box with baking soda before filling with litter.

Fill a stinky diaper pail with hot water and bleach (1 C bleach to 1 gallon hot water); let it stand for a few hours. Empty pail, rinse and dry. Rub inside with baking soda/water paste and let stand overnight. In the morning rinse the pail and it's ready to use. To prevent odors from returning sprinkle with baking soda and change water often.

To rid your hands of food odors, rub them with a paste of baking soda and water.

Use a paste of baking soda to clean away corrosion on car battery terminals without having to use a wire brush.

Use a solution of water and baking soda to clean and deodorize inside and around the door of your microwave.

Put a few spoonfuls in a cup of water in the microwave, boil for two minutes then wipe down the inside with a sponge.

Sprinkle a little baking soda into the laundry hamper to minimize odors from soiled clothing.

Dissolve 1/2 cup or more of baking soda in bathwater to soothe skin irritations from sunburn, insect bites, poison ivy and itchy rashes such as chicken pox or hives.

To remove black scuff marks from floor, rub them with a paste of baking soda and water. Use as little water as possible for the best results.

Clean fiberglass showers and tubs with baking soda sprinkled on a sponge. Sponge clean and wipe dry.

Soak sour smelling dishcloths and sponges in a water and baking soda solution to sweeten them up.

Add $1/3$ cup baking soda to a wash cycle as a bleach booster or to the rinse cycle for sweet, clean-smelling laundry.

If you have a septic tank (or RV holding tank) flush a cup of baking soda down the toilet periodically.

Remove coffee and tea stains by scrubbing pots or cups with baking soda and a plastic scouring pad.

Sprinkle a musty smelling ice chest with some baking soda and close the lid for an hour. Then rinse with clean water and wipe with a soft cloth dampened with a teaspoon of vanilla extract. Your ice chest will smell great between picnics.

Make a paste with water and rub on insect bites to relieve itchiness.

White Vinegar

To clear lime deposits out of faucets, put $1/3$ to $1/2$ cup vinegar in a plastic sandwich bag. Tie the bag to the faucet so the entire end is in the vinegar. Leave on for a couple of hours.

Use a vinegar and water solution to remove soapy film from countertops.

Put a few drops of vinegar in the water to help poached eggs hold their shape.

Boil hardened paint brushes in vinegar.

To remove wallpaper, mix equal parts vinegar and hot water. Dip a paint roller into the solution, wet the paper thoroughly. After two applications, most paper will peel off in sheets.

To assure your dishes come out sparkling clear with no soap or hard water residue, pour a cup of vinegar into dishwasher during final rinse.

Clean the hoses and unclog soap scum from your washing machine by pouring a gallon of distilled vinegar into it and running the machine through its entire cycle.

Wash your plastic shower curtain in the washing machine. Add 1 cup vinegar to the rinse cycle. Tumble dry with one or two towels.

Heat up some white vinegar on stove or in microwave. Use undiluted to wash down shower doors and any other area plagued by hard water marks and soap scum.

For beautiful azaleas, add two tablespoons of vinegar to a quart of water and use occasionally to water.

Pour white vinegar on unwanted grass in cracks and crevices or around sprinkler heads. It is safe, inexpensive and nontoxic.

Mop ceramic tile floors with hot water and vinegar solution only. No soap. They will shine and sparkle like new.

Fill a spray bottle or mister with vinegar to chase away ants.

Note: A pumice stone, available at any hardware store, is a very cheap but useful house-cleaning tool. The remarkable thing about a pumice stone is that it will quickly remove even the most stubborn stain from toilet or sink bowl—anything made of porcelain or ceramic tile—without scratching!

FREEZER TIPS

The best way to cut down on your food bill is to *stay out of the store!* How many times have you run off to the market just to pick up one item . . . and just happened to remember a few other things that you needed? And this or that looks so good and would be a great treat for later on . . . and before you know it that one item turns into a full cart.

If you're going to stay out of the store (except for those very occasional and well-planned trips), you're going to have to come up with a realistic way to store more food in the home. Because you will be buying in bulk and stocking up when items you use are on sale—a freezer should become a mandatory piece of equipment for a successful cheapskate life-style.

Your freezer, should you elect to get one, must fit into your financial plan, be placed conveniently close to the kitchen to insure its optimum use, and should be energy efficient so that you don't spend the money you save on running the thing.

A freezer is an item that is often available used and in pretty good condition. Just remember that the newer the model the more energy efficient it will be. For instance, we just recently purchased our first freezer. I was perfectly willing to consider a used one, but we found a new one on sale (with even a further reduction due to the dents and rumpled back corner), and with the newest mandatory energy efficiency, it will cost us only $56 a year to operate. We could have paid half the purchase price for an old inefficient freezer and ended up paying $250–$300 a year for additional electricity!

Frost-free models are more expensive up-front and use much more electricity. The regular type which requires defrosting is not much of a problem, however.

A great way to make sure that the door stays closed most of the time is to post an inventory sheet. That way you can peruse the contents, make your selection and limit the time the door is opened. Just be sure that you keep that list up-to-date and mark out an item as it is removed.

Home food freezing in small quantities is easy, pleasant and very much worth doing.

CASHING IN ON COUPONS
AND REFUNDS

I've tried. I've really tried. Halfheartedly? Haphazardly? Yes . . . but there have been many, albeit brief, occasions when my desire to achieve economic perfection has driven me to clip coupons. Without exception my intentions were always good. And without fail the neatly clipped critters would find their way into a remote compartment of my purse never to be seen again until a major clean-out would exile them to the throwaway pile. I admit that once in a very long while I've been known to remember some particular coupon and enjoy that righteous feeling as its double value was deducted from my total bill.

Over time I have come up with my own philosophy regarding coupons. They are ministers of clutter and guilt. It was a happy day when I embraced coupon liberation. My meaningless clipping ceased . . . that is until recently.

While flipping through the Sunday paper, I spotted a $1.00 off coupon for a particular hygienic product I buy regularly. Without missing a beat I ripped out that sucker, only to realize that a marvelous stroke of fate had given us two inserts—and I had two coupons! I grabbed my bag, went straight to the market, found the product . . . on sale . . . for $1.98. Sure I had two coupons, but there was no way I was going to get two items *free!* I actually worried about testing the process. What checker in his right mind would actually allow me to purchase two identical items with two coupons, double them and say I owed nothing? Hey, folks, I'm a pretty good cheapskate but I was embarking into unchartered territory and not feeling real comfortable. I engaged in a bit of self-talk, decided I was conducting a research project and boldly got in line.

Without even a moment's hesitation, the items were scanned, my coupons credited, tax was added and my total came to $.29! No security guards came running out, no one yelled over the loud speaker that some woman was trying to pull a fast one and the entire transaction was done clearly with their blessing.

Now all of you dyed-in-the-wool couponers out there: I have always admired your tenacity, but was determined that overall you could probably do better by dumping those coupon files of great poundage, stick to generic brands when at all possible and buy in bulk. But I couldn't get the case of the remarkable deodorant purchase out of my mind.

And so my inquiring mind drove me to the home of my friend Mary Ann Maring—a world-class couponer. (To tantalize you just a bit, Mary Ann not too long ago, had 160 boxes of ALL laundry detergent in her garage for which she paid only the cost of three boxes—clearly the most remarkable legal and ethical coupon feat of the century.) I had to get to the bottom of this.

The first thing I learned is that serious, profitable couponing is not for everyone. Certain personality types cannot tolerate the organizational rigors required to make couponing work. This activity if undertaken, must be done well—and that takes time; hours each and every week. It must be considered a part-time job requiring a commitment, patience and rigid determination.

For my fellow novices, there are two basic types of coupons. Manufacturer coupons and store coupons. In most areas there will be at least one supermarket which will double and occasionally triple these coupons. Store coupons, on the other hand, are typically good in one particular store only and are not doubled. I like to think of them as bait.

The Maring Method of Effective Couponing is to combine a doubled manufacturer's coupon with a store coupon on one single item. This is known as a double whammy; the ultimate, however, is the triple-whammy when the item is first of all on sale and you have both a store and doubled manufacturer's coupon. (Brings quite a rush so I understand.)

As my session continued, Mary Ann toured me through her coupon box; a medium-size green metal check filing box of considerable weight with tabbed dividers.

She has these labeled by categories, i.e., cereal, drinks, dairy, bakery, sauces, candy, laundry, cleaning, paper goods, etc. This is where she organizes and stores manufacturer's coupons which she collects from every source possible (magazines, newspapers, direct mail, grocery stores.)

Each Thursday and Sunday Mary Ann purchases a

local paper (her savings more than pays for the cost) and spends at least an hour going through the ads, noting the loss leaders and clipping the store coupons she will be able to use. Once she has determined the best buys for items she needs that week, she goes through the file to find any manufacturer coupons she can match up with the sales and/or store coupons. I found this confusing and tedious, but the light turned on when I applied the double and triple whammy techniques. There were many items for which she would pay only a few cents and occasionally she pointed out an item she would be getting absolutely *free*.

I would venture to say that Mary Ann had hundreds of coupons in her file, a file which is purged every four months. Expired coupons are thrown out (she has this activity down to such a science that not often will an expiration date get past her), soon-to-expire coupons are rotated to the front of their particular category and the total inventory is reassessed.

I was then invited to the garage where Mary Ann showed me her UPC file; large filing boxes divided into similar categories where product labels and grocery sales receipts are kept. These file boxes are the heartbeat of refunding. She showed me refund offers which require proofs of purchase (typically the proof accepted is the label including UPC code) and original sales receipts. Some of these refunds were for quite handsome amounts. Mary Ann is all prepared when she comes across a great refund. She doesn't have to run to the market, purchase 12 cans of bean soup, tear off the labels and force feed the soup to her family. She assesses the requirement, goes to the filing area, retrieves the box tops or labels necessary, matches up a sales receipt—pops it all into the mail and waits for the check!

The best part of the evening was when Mary Ann invited me to look through her record book. She has detailed records of the savings derived from coupons and refunds since 1980! Each month is tallied, each year totaled and as of December 31, 1991, this remarkable lady has saved solely with coupons and refunds a total of . . . are you ready? . . . $17,433.17! I was in shock. Remember, these are after tax funds. I saw this with my own eyes (which were nearly rolling back into my head by this time.) What percentage of this total represented purchases she would probably have not made had it not been for the coupons? She estimates about 30 percent but was quick to point out that such an item purchased eliminated the need to purchase an alternative or substitute. Her family has become adventurous eaters, willing to change brands without notice.

I have come to the conclusion that couponing/refunding is an excellent way to make one's grocery dollars go farther, but if attempted must be carried out in an excellent manner or this will surely become a spendy rather than thrifty activity.

Now that I have mercifully let some of you off the hook, let me challenge those who are fastidious and organized to take up couponing. This is a marvelous way to lower your grocery bill and eat better in the process and all the while feel satisfaction in contributing even more to the household income. I am so convinced of this that I have offered, and Mary Ann has agreed, to publish her complete and detailed couponing/refunding methods. I have found only a smattering of publications on this subject—most written ten to fifteen years ago and hopelessly out-of-date. Couponing in the nineties is a whole new ball game, and Mary Ann Maring is indeed the authority on the subject—right down to her tips on selecting the right grocery checker (an interesting technique). Watch for this booklet after the first of the year.

By the way—if you're wondering about the ALL laundry detergent story: Some time ago, Mary Ann noticed that the manufacturer was including a $1.00 off coupon on the side panel of a regular-size $1.99 box of ALL. She bought three boxes, clipped the coupons and the next week picked up three more boxes which she received free with the three $1.00 coupons which were doubled. (Her store would allow only three coupons for the same item at a time). She clipped those coupons (leaving the cardboard box intact) and repeated the process each week until the coupons were discontinued. I understand that at one time the top count was 160 boxes, the garage smelled great and every visitor to the Maring home cheerfully left with a box of ALL.

So am I persuaded to reconsider my position on coupons? Definitely yes. Will I ever be in a position to challenge the coupon queen to her throne? I seriously doubt it; but I believe that I can use some of her techniques to do even better with my food bill. I do have a new admiration and respect for the relatively few consumers who are truly effective couponers.

So if I pass one of you in the market (I'll recognize you because of that large filing cabinet in the front seat of the grocery cart), I promise to salute with great respect.

You may be an excellent candidate for coupon queen (or king) if you:

- Like organizing things
- Have tenacity and patience
- Can see the big picture
- Are flexible
- Enjoy a challenge
- Have a need to cut food costs
- Get a thrill from beating the system

If this describes you . . . then grab those scissors, get a respectable filing system and start clipping!

FRUGAL? YES! FRUMPY? NO!

There are some lengths to which I will not go. Period. For instance, I would rather go barefoot than wear tennis shoes held together with duct tape—as if that could ever be considered a realistic money-stretching technique!

Given the choice of having tacky, uncoordinated furniture or nothing at all, I'll opt for the latter every time. A personal standard perhaps, but that is the very reason I have learned to sew, paint, wallpaper, recover, redo and repair.

Outward appearance is evidence of the inward attitude. If you look good you feel good, and if you feel good you do good—and that goes for every area of life from your wardrobe (limited as it may be), to the atmosphere you create in your workplace and home.

Frugality has long been associated with frumpiness. A dowdy, disheveled appearance was the image I feared would be the inevitable result of living within some kind of financial constraint. I figured unbridled spending equaled antifrumpiness insurance. But that idea is nothing more than a myth! The pursuit of excellence is not financially dependent.

Style and Fashion. Keep up with what's "in" for your peer group. Not trendy or faddish, but "in"! Just because your 1970s plaid bell-bottoms still have some mileage left does not mean you should be wearing them. We don't care that the tuxedo you bought in 1962 has only been worn twice. It doesn't fit and nine-inch lapels and high-water pants are not becoming!

Never go to the supermarket in curlers (that goes for the women, too). And speaking of hair, it costs no more to have a contemporary coiffure than the style you wore ten years ago.

Keep your home decor fresh and current. Get rid of those dusty amber glass grapes sitting on the coffee table. Take a giant leap and paint the kitchen. Keeping up-to-date takes thought and creativity—not a lot of money. Your attitude will soar!

Clean and Neat. Soap and water are cheap. And clean is the finest look of all, from personal hygiene to your clothes, your car and your home. For heaven sakes, get rid of the engine block that's been sitting by your driveway for the last three years. No one believes it is the latest thing in creative planters, anyway. And those oil stains and puddles on your driveway—take a little time and clean them up. Elbow grease is *free!*

Cheapskates are often pack rats. We have thousands of potential uses for dumb things, don't we? Now honestly, do you really need all of the egg cartons piled in the garage or those stacks of tiny pieces of wood? Give it up!

If you haven't used it or worn it in the last year, get rid of it. When your church or club needs huge amounts of oddities like juice lids, plastic meat trays, and toilet paper tubes, they'll give you plenty of notice—and then they can find a place to store the stuff!

There is a certain dignity in simplicity. And just because something is a great bargain is not a good reason to buy it! Own only what you need or what brings incredible beauty to your life.

Confidentiality. Cheapskates find excellent bargains and our creativity often affords us unbelievable finds. But when you receive a compliment, graciously accept it instead of announcing all of the details. Let people assume your clothes are from Nordstrom if they want to. A heartfelt "thank you" as a response is not less honest than revealing the source and exact price! A little mystery as to how you are able to live so well on so little is quite dignified.

Balance. Don't let frugality take over. Life is a single-take with no rehearsal! Obsessive saving and self-denial is just as debilitating as obsessive spending and debting. Strike a balance. Make provisions for entertainment and fun. Do the things that bring you personal pleasure and joy! Cut down somewhere else that is less meaningful. Eat generic brands so you can afford season tickets to the theater. Do your own automobile maintenance and use the savings to buy your favorite perfume. Get creative and let your imagination run wild! Decide what for you is of very high priority and which areas really don't matter.

Then scrimp like crazy where it doesn't matter so you'll be able to indulge your highest desires. Surprisingly, the more you think in this direction, the fewer high priorities you will have, providing more areas where you won't mind cutting back.

GHOULS, GHOSTS AND CONSUMER DEBT: SCARY THINGS THAT CAN MAKE YOUR BLOOD RUN COLD

Have you noticed how very few topics these days are considered taboo? With so many talk shows clamoring to find something new I have concluded that people will discuss anything. Well, almost anything.

There is at least one holdout—a matter of great personal and private dimension. That is the subject of personal indebtedness. Millions and millions of persons (at least twenty million to be exact) at this moment are overwhelmed by the state their personal debt has created. And yet it seems that everywhere we turn more debt is being offered to us. And doesn't it look harmless? Buy now pay later! Thirty-six E-Z payments. Just three installments of $39.95. Don't fool yourself. Any kind of unsecured debt has a real potential to do you great harm.

Once you have established a life based on debting it is very hard to reverse the process! While not easy, the pattern of living with unsecured debt must be traded in for one of cash spending. It takes determination and total commitment and it can be done.

First of all, incurring any more new unsecured debt has to stop. Period. So what do you do when the refrigerator gives up the ghost and you have no cash? Or you suddenly realize the car needs new tires? Hopefully you will start now to plan for these things so you won't have to incur debt in order to survive.

Take your automobile, for example. It is foolish to think that you will never need new brakes or tires. By checking around a bit and reading the owner's manual you should be able to determine when these things are going to happen and what they will cost.

Let's say you determine that your brakes will be shot after 35,000 miles and the cost will be somewhere around $250. Since your car has 25,000 miles on it now and you drive approximately 12,000 miles a year, you can:

A. Determine that you have ten months to prepare. Or . . .

B. Hide your head in the sand and act surprised when you are faced with a terrible financial crisis next July.

Let's say you select Option A: $250 divided by 10 means you need to set aside $25 each month. Perhaps you won't need the brakes until August or September, but you will have the cash and the calmness of spirit to check around and find the best place to have the work done at a convenient time.

Option B on the other hand represents a much more complicated scenario: July comes and the brake pads are now the thickness of a heavy-duty trash bag. You are broke (what's new?) and pretend you don't hear the telltale sounds of metal against metal.

By the time you can stand it no longer the closest mechanic (you've lost the luxury of being able to shop around) determines that in addition to the $250 for brakes you need the rotors turned; an additional $75. Plus you will have to rent a car because this crisis has left you stranded. You charge the $325 brake bill and the $59 rental fee to your 19.6 percent Visa card. There's no way you can possibly pay it off in full during the first 30 days. You determine that you can pay $25 a month. You are now forced to set aside $25 a month even though you just "couldn't" 10 months ago!

If you faithfully pay the $25 a month, it will take you 17 months to pay off the debt. Total payback: $425 for what should have been a $250 brake job.

The worst part is that during the 17 months it takes you to pay for the brakes, you are not setting aside a similar amount for the next unforeseen emergency! Can you see how this debting thing is so injurious to your financial health? It gives you a false sense of security when in reality it is just setting you up for a worse catastrophe the next time around.

And chances are that in the case of Option B you would've found other "emergencies" to put on that Visa account increasing your balance and pushing your $0 balance day farther and farther into the future. Within a short time another case of perma-debt has been spawned.

So are you going to need another car in the next, let's say, ten years? Are any of your major appliances due for replacement any time soon? I know that it is not possible to establish cash reserves for every future major purchase overnight. But it is possible to start with one item. It is possible to stop incurring new debt and it is possible to get out of debt and stay out of debt!

MAY YOUR DAYS BE MERRY AND BRIGHT

You are riding through the snowy New England countryside in a sleigh pulled by a team of Clydesdale horses. The only sounds you can hear are the clippety-clop of horses' hooves and the jingling of sleigh bells. Your rosy cheeks are stinging slightly because of the rushing cold air. In the distance you see the glimmer of lights coming closer and your pulse speeds up just a bit as the sound of "I'll Be Home for Christmas" comes ever so slightly through the trees. The anticipation of hot cider and seeing friends and loved ones who are waiting ahead assures you this will be the most perfect Christmas ever.

Sound good? I've just described my own Christmas fantasy and I have a feeling you wouldn't turn down an experience like that either. After all, don't we all long for a serene, less commercialized holiday?

If Christmas means joy, why does it cause so much anxiety? If the message of the season is peace on earth, goodwill to men, then why do increasingly more people find themselves propelled into a season of depression and "the blues"? How could something so simple, so beautiful turn into a 30-billion-dollar-a-year commercial extravaganza? Invariably we end up spending money we don't have to buy gifts which are neither liked nor wanted. And the worst part is that it will probably take until next year at this time to pay off the debt. Something has gone wrong—terribly wrong!

To say that Christmas has become our national neurosis is probably an understatement. Show me a head clerk in a typical toy store today and I'll show you a crazy person come 6:00 P.M. on December 24.

With all of the hype over corporate forecasts and profit margins one would think our entire economic system teeters precariously on the population's propensity to Buy! Shop! Charge! Spend! And doesn't Wall Street get nervous when their indicators start to decline?

Already the media is blitzing us with offers of "90-days deferred payment," "No payments until next year," leading us to believe that the higher the price tag the happier the recipient. Do we really believe that we can buy love and happiness? Remember: the more desperate the times the more creative the scams.

Do you ever dread the month of December knowing that you will be required to transform your family's every day life into a beautiful magical festival by planning, organizing, host and hostessing, decorating, shopping, housecleaning, cooking, baking and refereeing? Most of us are used to being so busy that we don't even have time to question what we're doing.

Let me suggest that there is a better way. We must take back control that Madison Avenue and American Express have stripped from us. Maybe, just maybe, we can restore the simplicity and beauty of the season and come out on December 26 with our spirits high, our bank accounts intact and our credit cards with a zero balance. It won't be easy, but perhaps our children's obsession with brand-name toys can be turned into joyous anticipation and wonder for the miracle of the season. Maybe we won't have to compete for the title of Christmas Magician anymore!

Here's what the experts tell us that research has determined the average person really wants for Christmas.

1. Relaxed loving time with family
2. Realistic expectations about gifts
3. An evenly paced holiday season
4. Strong family traditions

The same research determined that the greatest need of all children at Christmas—just like any time of the year—is the assurance that they are very much wanted and loved by their parents. Doesn't that sum up what we all need—to be wanted and loved by those closest to us?

But what usually happens in December? This is

the one month when the calendar is crammed full, spare time being the rarest commodity of all. Families are usually scattered as their lives become crowded with church rehearsals, benefits, shopping trips, parties, concerts and social events. And any time spent at home is usually preoccupied with holiday chores, plans, and the big one . . . money worries.

I would like to suggest that spending time with your family and your children is so important that it might be prudent to consider turning down social invitations, traveling and performances as necessary to allow for this important priority.

Try to recall Christmases past. What were the things you wish you would have made time for? Who are the people you wish you would have visited? Which jigsaw puzzles did you intend to put together but are still gathering dust? Wish you had the courage to let the kids decorate the tree any way they want? Well, guess what? You have an opportunity to get it right this year.

So right now make a decision to slow down, relax, stay home more and spend less. Who knows? Maybe you'll figure out how to pack up the kids, engage a team of Clydesdales, jump in a sleigh and listen to the silence of snow falling instead of the mall calling.

Come January 2 you'll be glad you did. And let me be the first to wish you a refreshing and joyous holiday—Merry Christmas and Happy Chanukah!

TRADITIONS: MEMORIES
IN PROCESS

Tradition . . . it's the tea in which Christmas is steeped. Tradition gives Christmas its deep, rich color . . . its warming memories . . . its satisfying aftertaste.

Traditions give children and adults alike great comfort and security and bring back memories of all the Christmases that have gone before.

Very simple activities can satisfy the need for tradition. Kids perceive anything they can count on from year to year as a tradition and most families have more of these hidden rituals than they realize.

Consider instituting some new traditions around your house this year. Maybe all you need is a little push. My friend Kathleen Chapman is the one who taught me all about traditions. Here are some ideas to get your creative juices flowing:

Pick out the tree on the same day every year. Go to the same place in the forest or the same lot every year.

Select a special hot drink or snack item which will always be associated with trimming the tree.

Allow each child individually to miss one day of school during December to spend the day all alone with Mom or Dad. Let the child plan the day. Suggestions: Christmas shopping, baking cookies.

Prepare the same menu every Christmas Eve.

Make a Christmas video every year. Have your world premiere on Christmas Eve.

Play the same Christmas tapes year after year starting the minute Thanksgiving is over.

Establish a time to visit special friends.

Go Christmas caroling to the same places on the same day, year after year.

The first person up on Christmas morning is required to start the music and light the fire!

The whole family attends services together on Christmas Eve.

Decorate the outside of the house the same every year.

Pick a special breakfast menu which is reserved for Christmas morning only. You'll spoil the tradition if you serve it other times of the year.

Read the same stories at a certain appointed time.

A gingerbread house made from scratch every Christmas can be a family project.

Place a game table in the same place every year with a jigsaw puzzle in process. Establish a tradition that it must be finished before midnight on Christmas Eve.

Reserve one special ornament to top the tree every year without fail.

Now add one more tradition to your list. Renew your subscription to *Cheapskate Monthly* on the same day every year. Let me know about your own traditions and any that you start this year. I'll save them up for the Holiday Issue next year. It'll be a tradition!

MAKE YOUR OWN HOLIDAY CARDS!

Have you checked out the ever increasing price of Christmas and Chanukah cards this year? You might think about making your own.

You may even want to consider having your special holiday card double for a gift. You will surely accomplish this goal if your card has lasting significance: a family picture, poem, story, original song or painting. Don't you love receiving those kinds of special cards?

Try your hand at the Family Christmas Letter. You want to send a detailed note about the previous year's goings-on, but haven't the time or the energy to write 75 times about the master's thesis, the new baby or your triumph climbing Mt. Whitney. Not many people will share the desire for a lengthy epistle, but a light and witty page of family news, ideas, and happenings usually is welcomed by good friends and relatives. If you don't think you are capable of witty, just write in conversational style as if you were talking over the phone.

Your local quick printer will have holiday stationery on which you can either photocopy or have your creation offset printed.

A book by Edna Barth, *A Christmas Feast* (Houghton Mifflin/Clarion Books) is full of whimsical Christmas poetry, wishes and greetings, and should be a rich source from which to draw lines for your homemade cards.

An artist in the family? Start yet another tradition

by reproducing an original picture for your cards. If that artist is a child how fun it will be for those on your list to see the growth and improvement each year!

Years ago, a modern composer named Alfred Burt, wrote a Christmas carol each year and sent original copies of it as the family's Christmas greeting. Not only was this a unique idea, he was a very talented composer who hit it big. Now, hopefully the recipients hung on to those copies because they are extremely valuable. Maybe you are one of the lucky ones who has an original of "Caroling, Caroling," "We'll Dress the House" or "Some Children See Him!"

GIFTS FROM THE HEART

Contrary to popular belief, the quality of a gift is not measured by the digits in the price tag. A pricey item given out of obligation cannot hold a candle to a gift of the heart. It is not too late to come up with some terrific ways that you can give of yourself this holiday season.

Last May I received a wonderful letter from subscriber Clover Behrend. Included was the following which I have been patiently holding for this issue. I immediately came up with some ideas of my own because Clover's list put me into a creative mode. Hopefully the same will happen for you.

"In a society quite dedicated to conspicuous consumption and material possessions, my friends tell me I have a refreshing approach to gift giving. Instead of wracking my brain to find a material gift, I give an 'experience' or a 'service' that I know my friend either wants or would not do for himself/herself. These gifts truly come from the heart and usually involve interaction of a personal nature. I buy a card and make up a 'coupon' redeemable at my friend's convenience. Some suggestions:

1. A few hours of running errands.
2. Shuttle service to and from an airport.
3. A wonderful massage (I am a masseuse, so I do it myself, but a gift certificate for a massage elsewhere would work, too).
4. Mom and Dad's Day Off. I take their children for a day of fun.
5. Any number of homemade goodies, from beef jerky to pies and cakes for their special event (redeemable with a few days' notice).
6. A small box into which I put 30 little notes, each indicating a small, wonderful, relaxing activity my friend can enjoy. Each day for a month he/she takes out a slip and completes the activity. Activities are limited only by what you know are your friend's tastes (though throwing in a 'risky' thing can be fun): 'Go outside and walk in the grass, barefooted'; 'Take a one-hour relaxing soak in the tub'; 'Pick one chore you plan to do today, don't do it, and read a chapter in your favorite book

instead.' In our rush rush world we too often don't take time to do such things because our silly subconscious stuff doesn't allow it. All we need is 'permission,' and this gift somehow gives that permission! (This is one of my favorites.)

7. A day of general repair service.

8. A donation in your friend's name to one of their favorite charities. (Last Christmas we made a donation in a friend's name to the Los Angeles Mission, and they said it was the best Christmas gift they had ever received.)

9. Make a long list of the ways your friend has positively impacted your life. Write or type your list on paper and give it. (I did this for my dad for a Father's Day gift when I was 37—e.g., 'I appreciate the way you taught me the value of money,' 'I appreciate that you took pictures of me while I was growing up and I enjoy looking at them,' etc. My dad wept upon reading it, then gave me the biggest hug I'd ever had.)

10. An empty envelope with a note that says, 'Hey, bet you think you're not getting a gift! This envelope contains magic. Each time you hold it, know I'm thinking fond thoughts of you and that I'm here for you whenever you need me'—or something to that effect.

11. Any other 'gift from the heart.' One is limited only by imagination!

"The nice thing about such gifts is that planning them is as much fun as receiving them. I really think the secret is to disengage from the 'traditional' idea of going to a store to purchase a gift, and have the courage to do something different from what you may have done all your life. It was with a bit of trepidation that I gave my first 'not bought gift,' but the response was so positive that I vowed to always 'give an experience' rather than a store-bought gift. My husband and I have not given a material gift in many years, and our friends love the experiences we've given."

Thank you, Clover.

CHAPTER 8

Selected Reader Mail

From the first day that *Cheapskate Monthly* started its way around the country, I've been receiving dozens and dozens of wonderful letters. Some of them make me laugh, some have made me cry, all have encouraged me and some have even made me bristle a bit. But every single one has been lovingly read, reread, answered if necessary, taken under advisement and filed away under the most unusual of categories. Here's a sampling.

"Dear Mary,

"Your newsletter has made such a difference in my life. Since subscribing just a few short months ago, I am so much more cognizant and careful in my spending. I am on Week 3 of recording every penny I spend and can't wait to make out my own

personalized spending plan. My 'coma' days are over and I am finally in control of my finances.
Mary DeCarlo"

"Dear Mary,

"I would like to thank you for the excellent newsletter called *Cheapskate Monthly*. Having been an accountant for over twenty years, I am impressed with the articles on budgeting and spending money wisely. Over the years I have tried to educate my clients about the importance of budgeting, but your firsthand experience adds credibility and is reflected in your articles.
Kenneth I. Kubota"

"Dear C.M.,

"I've got a great idea for a birthday party . . . for less than $10.00!

"Our teenage daughter and several of her friends wanted to 'throw' an extra special birthday party for one of their other friends . . . however none of them had any money! Here's what we came up with:

"All 16 of them piled into cars and headed for the largest mall in the area, armed only with a camera and a roll of film.

"They proceeded to walk the mall . . . store by store selecting gifts for the birthday girl that they would like to buy her, if they had the money. But instead of buying the item . . . they took a picture of themselves with the gift and the birthday girl.

"They went to the finest stores and were very polite with the salespersons who really got into it and allowed them to photograph furs, expensive jewelry, etc.

"When the evening was over the pictures were developed and the birthday girl had a photo album to parallel none other, not to mention the 'hit' party of the year!
Kathleen Chapman"

"Dear Mary Hunt,

"I have to quit showing my notebook of *Cheapskate Monthly* issues around . . . it's costing me money. Here is a check to cover another subscription and the back issues. At a recent social event at which I just happened to have them at hand, several people took down your address and said they wanted to subscribe also. You've really hit on something great. Thanks for your fine newsletter and very quick service. I don't know how you do it! Keep up the good work.
Margaret Charles"

"Dear Mary,

"Me, too, cheap all the way although I prefer to name this procedure 'Good Management Skills.'
Marty Delman"

"Dear Mary,

"Your newsletter gives new hope to the otherwise indigent spender. We can all learn valuable lessons

on how to make the most from next to nothing. Thank you for your foresight and concern for those of us who wish to share your values and quality of life. Your guidance and helpful hints are so welcomed.
Debra Smith"

"Dear Ms. Hunt,

"I need help in order to save myself from myself. I am a spending addict and am so glad to learn about your newsletter. Enclosed is my check for a one-year subscription. Hopefully, it will not bounce.

A clear indication that my addiction has worsened is that I used to buy for myself. Now I buy stuff and have to find people to give the items to. Believe it or not I am a relatively intelligent woman and I earn $50,000 a year. A trip to the store is financial roulette for me. I never know what or how much I will buy.

"I really hope you will be able to help me.
Name withheld"

"Dear Mary,

"I'm so impressed with my first copy of CM! Not only am I impressed with its content and the presentation, but I received it only a week after I sent my subscription check—along with probably hundreds of others. Of particular interest was your story and I just love your natural, down-home style of writing. Makes me feel like a close friend is writing this news-

letter (and I guess that's quite true, isn't it?). Keep up your wonderful work on behalf of us proud 'Cheapskates'!
Clover Behrend"

Suggested Reading and Additional Help

I would highly recommend the following books. I received great help and encouragement from them and you might, too. Check with your local library. If not immediately available ask about their interlibrary loan policies. I have included publisher addresses for workbooks.

Mundis, Jerrold
How to Get Out of Debt, Stay Out of Debt and Live Prosperously
Bantam 1988

Okholm, Huntley
Money Mastery Workbook; Budget Friend or Foe?
R.C. Law Publishers
c/o 1245 #88 W. Cienega Ave.
San Dimas, CA 91773

Avanzini, John
Rapid Debt-Reduction Strategies
HIS Publishing Company
P.O. Box 1096
Hurst, TX 76053

Clason, George S.
The Richest Man in Babylon
Signet 1988

Arenson, Gloria
Born to Shop
TAB Books 1991

The following are nonprofit organizations that offer help and hope in the area of credit and debt problems. You can call for information without obligation.

Debtors Anonymous
General Service Board
P.O. Box 20322
New York, NY 10025-9992
(212) 642-8222

The National Foundation for Consumer Credit
(a.k.a. Consumer Credit Counseling Services)
(800) 388-2227

Believe me—they've heard of situations much worse than yours (mine for example) so don't be afraid to call! Your anonymity will be protected.

A Final Word

While I'm sure I have only scratched the surface of the whole idea of living financially responsible in a very financially irresponsible world, I hope that you have been encouraged to get started spending less, saving and giving more . . . and for heaven's sake —stay out of debt! I know you'll come up with thousands of other ways to cut expenses that I've never even thought of. (I know that's hard to believe!) And when you do, you've just got to let me in on it. Drop me a line and let me know if I can share it with all of the cheapskate family. I promise to make it worth your trouble.

It's time . . . go . . . now . . . take on the world!

❄ HERE'S HOW

HOW TO BUY A CAR by James R. Ross
The essential guide that gives you the edge in buying a new or used car.
_____ 95151-5 $4.99 U.S./$5.99 Can.

TAKING CARE OF CLOTHES: An Owner's Manual for Care, Repair and Spot Removal by Mablen Jones
The most comprehensive handbook of its kind...save money—and save your wardrobe!
_____ 90355-3 $4.95 U.S.   _____ 90356-1 $5.95 Can.

THE OFFICIAL HARVARD STUDENT AGENCIES BARTENDING COURSE (Trade Paperback)
All the essentials of a $300 professional bartending course, plus job-hunting techniques and money-making strategies
_____ 11370-6 $9.95 U.S.

KNITTING WITH DOG HAIR (Trade Paperback)
A Warp-to-Woof Guide to Making Scarves, Sweaters, Mittens & Much More
_____ 10489-8 $9.95 U.S.

EXPERT CHILD-CARE ADVICE AND HELP—

from St. Martin's Paperbacks

———— ❦ ————

FAMILY RULES
Kenneth Kaye, Ph.D.
Here's how to custom-design a straightforward set of rules on discipline that will fit *your* family.
_____ 95220-1 $5.99 U.S./$6.99 Can.

THE FIRST FIVE YEARS
Virginia E. Pomeranz, M.D., with Dodi Schultz
The classic guide to baby and child care, including answers to the 33 most-asked questions.
_____ 90921-7 $3.99 U.S./$4.99 Can.

BABY SIGNALS
Diane Lynch-Fraser, Ed.D., and Ellenmorris Tiegerman, Ph.D.
There are four distinct styles which infants communicate with—and this book tells you what they are and how to respond.
_____ 92456-9 $3.99 U.S./$4.99 Can.

CHILD CARE BOOKS
YOU CAN
COUNT ON—

from ST. MARTIN'S PAPERBACKS

BEYOND JENNIFER AND JASON
Linda Rosenkrantz and Pamela Redmond Satran
Newly updated, this landmark book is truly the only guide
you'll need to naming your baby!
_____ 95444-1 $4.99 U.S./$5.99 Can.

GOOD BEHAVIOR
Stephen W. Garber, Ph.D., Marianne Daniels Garber, and
Robyn Freedman Spizman
This comprehensive, bestselling guide lists answers to over
a thousand of the most challenging childhood problems.
_____ 95263-5 $6.99 U.S./$7.99 Can.

THE SELF-CALMED BABY
William A.H. Sammons, M.D.
Strung-out babies *can* calm themselves—and this one-of-
a-kind guide shows you how to help them do it!
_____ 92468-2 $4.50 U.S./$5.50 Can.